Acoustic
GUITAR MAKING
The Steel String Guitar

Acoustic GUITAR MAKING

The Steel String Guitar

Nick Blishen

THE CROWOOD PRESS

First published in 2012 by
The Crowood Press Ltd
Ramsbury, Marlborough
Wiltshire SN8 2HR

www.crowood.com

© Nick Blishen 2012

British Library Cataloguing-in-Publication Data
A catalogue record for this book is available from the British
Library.

ISBN 978 1 84797 374 0

Typeset by Servis Filmsetting Ltd, Stockport, Cheshire
Printed and bound in Malaysia by Times Offset (M) Sdn Bhd

CONTENTS

Acknowledgements   6

Foreword   7

Preface: How It All Started   9

Introduction   10

---

1   Materials and Equipment   15

2   The Anatomy of the Steel-String Guitar   35

3   Making the Component Parts   39

4   Assembling the Component Parts of the Body   87

5   Assembling the Neck, Fingerboard and Fretting   113

6   Finishing   147

7   Setting Up   155

A Note From the Author   166

Glossary   168

Suggested Further Reading   170

Suppliers   172

Index   174

ACKNOWLEDGEMENTS

I'd like to thank the following, in no particular order. My wife, for her enormous patience and understanding, and for putting up with the fact that the kitchen has not been finished for yet another year. Harry Collins, who first taught me woodwork, and the importance of the 'planing rules'. Student Andrew Witkowski for helping with the making of Guitar #2. Malcolm Prior, who unlocked a lot of the mysteries behind instrument-making for me. All of my students and the technicians for their encouragement, and for the odd cup of coffee and Jammie Dodger (the things some people will do to get an acknowledgement). My much-missed Father, who, as a teacher and writer himself, would have been proud of what I have finally achieved. My Mother, for her tireless encouragement. To the memory of our much-beloved Oscar, a cat who was an enormous part of our lives, who also supplied that one hair which would linger in the atmosphere long enough to settle on the 'last' coat of varnish, as an eternal reminder of what is important in life. My good friend Bob Luck for the loan of his Stratocaster. My brother Jon Blishen for proofreading and pulling me up on my grammar and spelling as only an English teacher can. My friend and guitarist extraordinaire Steve Walters for proofreading and timely comments. My friends and fellow makers Malcolm Prior, Norman Myall, Martin Bowers, Godefroy Mauejouls and Hugh 'Chip' Chipperfield for their brilliant quotes, although some took a lot of nagging, cajoling and threats to obtain.

FOREWORD

The following are comments from friends, colleagues and fellow instrument makers. I hope you will find them inspirational!

Creating musical instruments from a material as unpredictable and capricious as wood requires patience and tenacity, as well as technical skill and a sense of creativity. There is an almost endless fascination to be had from making an object that combines visual beauty with a unique voice. In the Renaissance the highest praise that a sculptor could receive was that their work 'lacked only breath' – as instrument makers we can make wood speak, and therein lies the reward. On the practical side I have always loved being in the environment of a well-equipped workshop. There are the pleasures of using good, well-set hand tools, and working interesting and beautiful timbers. For the alchemist within me, there is all the fascination of making and applying varnish, pigments and glues that are as useful and relevant now as they were five hundred years ago.

On the creative side, all of this material skill and knowledge has to be guided by a secure knowledge of instrument design and theory. When all these things are put together, and an instrument is finished, even minor complications along the way are forgotten, and one is left with a sense of reward and achievement that is hard to beat.

Malcolm Prior (lute maker and former tutor)

Important influences in my career as an instrument maker come from my parents' interest in music, an education in the arts and playing the music of Renaissance and baroque composers on the guitar and lute from an early age.

For me there are few things more motivating and creative than making a beautifully shaped, proportioned and sounding musical instrument from start to completion: researching

the requirements of an instrument for the client, using my experience and skills selecting and preparing the timbers and varnish, then carving and sculpting the living materials, 'bringing the instrument out of the wood', mysteriously each one having its own unique sound and characteristics.

After many hours of meticulous work, the instrument is launched into the wide world and I am rewarded by following its development as it matures, hearing the sound and tone grow in the hands of the player bringing pleasure to the musician and audience.

Martin Bowers (instrument maker, restorer and repairer, former tutor)

As a child coming from a musical family I grew up surrounded by instruments and I became fascinated by their shape and design. A Cabinet Making Apprenticeship led me to a course in Instrument Making and gave me the opportunity to make guitars and other stringed instruments. I found I had an affinity with this craft of lutherie and, after thirty-five years of making and teaching, I am amazed and pleased that I am still learning and evolving my style while being influenced by every good instrument I see. The best thing about making for me is the satisfaction of seeing the instrument I have lovingly created being enjoyed and played by others.

Norman Myall (instrument maker, tutor)

I just love coming in the morning, smelling the various odours in the workshop, handling the tools, looking at those shapes and colours that make a guitar. I love spending long moments looking at the figure in a piece of wood and deciding how to cut it in order to show at best its natural splendour – sometimes spending even longer to get a joint or shape as close to perfection as possible. I love finishing a guitar, stringing it up and playing it for the next few days and feeling the sound growing in it, to then see the same guitar one year, two years down the line and appreciate how it has opened up ... These are some of the many reasons why I do this job of making guitars ... the simple love of the instrument and of the craft.

Godefroy Maruejouls (guitar maker, evening class tutor)

The reason I love making guitars is due to having spent most of my working life making component parts for furniture makers, interior designers and architects, and very rarely seeing the finished work. Therefore, it is a real joy to make a guitar from scratch. Although I find every stage really enjoyable, the most exciting part is the final set-up and putting the strings on. The reward after hours of work is the thrill of hearing it come to life.

Hugh 'Chip' Chipperfield (woodturner, guitar and mandolin maker)

The author subjecting Guitar #1 (described in this book) to some soulful blues.

Cutaway on Guitar #1.

PREFACE: HOW IT ALL STARTED

Way back in the dim and distant past, when Bert Weedon was persuading us that we could play in a day, and Bill Haley was rocking around his clock, the seeds were sown and my fascination with guitars began. Little can I have known, however, when I was joyfully bashing out tunes on a plastic Tommy Steele instrument, that one day guitars would become such a major part of my life.

Fast-forward three decades and I was stuck in a job I didn't want to do, staring redundancy in the face. I had worked in a music shop after leaving college, but then I had to get a 'proper job' and worked in the electronics industry for over twenty years. The various positions I managed to persuade successive employers that I was capable of holding included prototype wireman, test engineer and design draughtsman. So here I was, sitting at a drawing board, being berated for not wearing a tie and generally making the office look untidy.

As rumours spread that half the workforce were going to lose their jobs, I had a eureka moment. I'd discovered a guitar-making course at the City of London Polytechnic (formerly the London College of Furniture) and decided that it was now or never – to combine my love of music, woodwork and guitars, and live happily ever after.

I studied at the college for four years (it had in the meantime been renamed the London Guildhall University) and then set up my own workshop in the Hertfordshire/Essex border area. After a few years of making and repairing guitars the University (now once again renamed, this time the London Metropolitan University) asked me to teach their guitar-making evening class. This was followed by teaching a day a week on the degree course, and I find myself currently running the BSc Musical Instruments and teaching guitar-making to a succession of eager newcomers to the profession.

The author's wife Lorna putting Guitar #2 through its paces.

INTRODUCTION

(The use of **bold type** indicates terms that are explained in full in the glossary at the end of this book.)

Why Would You Want to Make Your Own Guitar?

A vast number of people are happy to buy a mass-produced guitar and, it has to be acknowledged, a lot of the time these instruments fulfil the player's needs. However, there are those amongst us who have tried a few different models and start to think, 'wouldn't it be good to have the body shape of that one, the neck profile from this one, the bass response of that, the finish from this …' – you get the idea? It could be that the instrument you have always lusted after has a vintage price tag that puts it out of reach of us mere mortals and has become the preserve of the professional collector. You may even suffer the same frustration I do, of trying to find a suitable left-handed version. Well, wouldn't it be good to have the guitar that you have always wanted, along with the satisfaction that you achieved it all by yourself?

The Uniqueness of Your Own Handmade Instrument

Even if you follow a proven design closely, there are plenty of opportunities to make your instrument unique. There is a fairly large choice of materials available that are suitable for instrument-making, so instead of using rosewood why not try walnut, or even pink ivory? The **soundhole inlay** can be redesigned to your own taste, and the **purfling**, **finger-board** and **binding** can be installed in contrasting woods of different colours. Even the finish can make a big difference to the look of your instrument. If you look at the two guitars in this book, although they are based on a **000-style twelve-fret**, they look very different from each other. Apart from the obvious variation that one is left-handed and the other right-handed, the different woods, **headstock** type, soundhole inlay and cutaway all go to personalize each instrument.

The Difference Between Factory-Made and Luthier-Made/Bespoke Instruments

Mass-produced instruments are generally made to a formula. As the name implies, the components for these instruments are made on a production line, with all parts fabricated in an identical fashion, commonly by machine. Guitars made in this way can be extremely good, and more often than not satisfy a player's needs. However, they are built in such a way that they will stand up to the rigours of performance, touring and general abuse (certainly during the guarantee period). Consequently, they are sometimes over-built, with thicker than necessary **soundboard**s and heavy durable finishes that can be detrimental to the overall sound and their playability.

As wood is an organic material, no two pieces will behave in exactly the same way or have identical characteristics. For instance, two soundboards even made from the same tree and put through the same thicknessing machine can end up being different in terms of stiffness, grain orientation, grain straightness and number of grain lines per inch – all attributes that can affect the soundboard's ability to resonate, enhance or even dampen certain frequencies and so on. This goes some way to explain why you can walk into a music shop, play several identical instruments and one will often stand out as being significantly different.

The job of a **luthier** (the term commonly used to describe a maker of stringed instruments), however, is to recognize the characteristics of each individual piece of timber and to get the optimum performance. For example, rather than working to a fixed formula, the thickness of each soundboard is determined from the knowledge that a stiff piece can be worked thinner than a less stiff piece.

Deciding Which Model of Guitar Suits Your Style of Playing

The whole subject of whether the sound of a particular guitar is better than another is fairly subjective. One man's eternally resonant and responsive instrument can be another man's nightmare, so before you embark on this incredible journey, you need to establish what style or model of guitar you want to build. The most obvious answer is to try many 'off the peg' instruments of different styles to ascertain which model type suits you. The following will hopefully help you to narrow down the search for your ultimate instrument.

Physical Attributes

It is important that the instrument you play is compatible with you. The size and depth of the guitar's body, the location of the **waist**, the length and width of the neck, string length and string tension all combine to result in an instrument that either you enjoy playing with ease (notwithstanding your ability to hold down a tune) or is a monster that leaves you with tense and aching limbs. Any pain of this sort caused by playing an instrument should be taken seriously, as in the long term it can lead to permanent damage to ligaments and muscles.

If you are going to be sitting down to play, consider the position of the instrument's waist, and how this affects access to the neck. A waist or centre-bout that is high up the body profile will bring the neck closer to you, and could make your fretting hand more comfortable.

If you are going to be standing with the guitar on a strap, think about how the depth and size of the body affects the positioning of the neck and therefore your fretting hand. The overall weight of the instrument should also be taken into consideration.

If you are relatively small of build, and have always lusted after a jumbo-sized guitar, this could end up being an unhappy marriage. With their generally large depth and body size, these types of instruments can lead to arms 'going to sleep' due to decreasing blood circulation, and the setting in of cramp and strain due to over-reaching.

Model Type

Parlour This type of guitar is currently enjoying a resurgence in popularity. Long favoured by 'blues' guitarists due to its sound and relative portability, it is going through a bit of a renaissance with finger-style players due to its 'sweet' tone, short scale length and lighter string tension. This, coupled with the availability of good pickup and microphone systems, has made players realize that you don't need a huge guitar to get yourself heard.

Grand Auditorium A good all-rounder, suitable for both strumming and finger-picking. This has a good balance of tone – that is, it doesn't suffer from a predominance of either bass or treble.

Grand Symphony Slightly larger than the Grand Auditorium, this is suitable for players who like to 'dig in' and drive the instrument hard without losing note definition.

Grand Concert Although a smaller bodied instrument, this type is capable of 'cutting through the mix', so would be good for recording. It favours tone over volume and is suited to finger-style playing.

Dreadnought A large guitar with a strong bass response but not a large amount of sustain. This type is generally favoured by strummers and flat-pickers. Often square-shouldered with a wide waist.

Jumbo As its name suggests, these are amongst the biggest guitars available, deep bodied with tighter waists. This type is again favoured by strummers due to its big sound and booming bass.

Woods

The different woods used in the making of an instrument affect the sound and tone depending on their characteristics. As it is generally agreed that the soundboard is the most vital component in the guitar's construction, the following list gives details of some of the **tonewoods** commonly employed. Although they are generalizations, they may go some way to help you tailor your guitar to the sound you desire.

Sitka spruce The most popular and favoured soundboard tone wood used by guitar makers due to the fact that it is strong but flexible, with a broad dynamic range. Suitable for the more aggressive player, and with a very good weight-to-strength ratio.

Engelmann spruce Some prefer the tone of this wood, which is generally considered slightly mellower and more 'mature' than Sitka. This probably sits between Sitka and Cedar. It is not as readily available as Sitka.

Western red cedar Once the preserve of 'classical' guitars, this is now becoming more common on steel string instruments. It is generally regarded as giving a warm and mellow tone compared to spruce, with a quick response that responds well to a light touch.

Hardwoods See discussion on rosewoods and alternative woods in 'Woods Traditionally Used' in the 'Materials' section of Chapter 1.

You may have already decided what you are going to build, but now want to know where to get the details and plans for making it. See the List of Suppliers, in which you will find details of working drawings that cover many, if not all, the models mentioned above.

This book will show you how to make a 000-style twelve-fret guitar, and any cutting list or dimensions will relate to that instrument. If you decide to make an alternative model, however, you may need to amend the sizes of timber to suit. Whatever model of steel-string guitar you decide upon, they can be constructed using the method that follows.

Luthiery Essentials

1. Sharpness is Key

I have this phrase written up in the workshop where I teach. It really cannot be stressed enough. Any good woodworker will tell you that you can not ignore this vital principle. In brief,

honing plane blades, chisels and scrapers to be as sharp as possible will help to ensure that instrument-making is a joyful experience (*see* 'Sharpening' in Chapter 1 for an in-depth description of good technique). It will avoid undoing hours of hard work in one careless stroke and will make you proud of the resultant finish, which you wouldn't originally have thought possible.

Because this is so important, throughout this book I frequently use phrases such as 'use a very sharp scraper' or 'a very sharp chisel', for which I make no apologies.

2. Sharpen Often

Set up a sharpening/honing station that is always accessible and ready to use. This way you will be encouraged to sharpen frequently and not be tempted to use a blunt tool because it is too much trouble to search out the honing equipment.

Getting into the habit of re-sharpening a tool before you use it really does pay dividends. It is all too easy to remember that you sharpened it only yesterday but to forget how much work you did with it in the interim.

With practise, the sharpening process will become so easy and automatic that you will not think twice about doing it.

3. Patience

Try not to rush a job, especially when you have that spare moment when you try to fit in a bit of making; this is when things normally go wrong. Don't think of guitar-making as a race against time. More often than not, slow and deliberate work is more efficient (with fewer careless mistakes and less re-making) and far more rewarding.

4. Planning

Although I have set out the making process in what I would consider a logical sequence of events, there may be certain components you wish to make, or a gluing procedure, that you can fit into your schedule at a particular time. Try and plan this work so that you get the maximum benefit from the time you have allotted. If you have glued and clamped a set of components, for example, do it at a time when you can leave it for the recommended duration. In other words, have another task lined up so that you won't be tempted to unclamp the work after a short time because it is holding up progress (*see* 'Gluing' below).

5. Gluing

Do a dry run before applying glue. This is essential when using animal-based glue. Due to the fact that this type of glue sets extremely quickly, you have no time to waste scrabbling around the workshop for that extra clamp. Even if you have decided to use a synthetic glue, which will generally have a much longer 'open time', having everything set up and ready will reduce the possibility of things going wrong.

When components are clamped and glued, don't be tempted to unclamp them too soon. Follow the relevant glue manufacturer's recommendations, but if you are at all unsure then leave the work overnight and get on with another job in the meantime.

6. Light

Always work in good light, preferably natural daylight, but if it has to be electric light, use daylight bulbs. This will help to reveal tool marks and rough or torn wood surfaces and will inspire you to try to achieve the best finish that you can.

7. Perfection

Don't try and strive for perfection, especially when you are starting out. You will make mistakes on your first instruments, but as long as you have patience and are willing to remake a component to replace a part that went wrong or that you are not happy with, things will get better and you will learn all the time. Remember this mantra: 'It's only a disaster if you learn nothing from it'.

If you intend, as I hope you will, to go on to make more instruments, by accepting that your first attempt is not going to be perfect you will have the opportunity on subsequent guitars to improve on what you have already done and learnt.

Having said all of that, try not to get into the habit of thinking, 'Oh, that will do'. A bit of extra work fine-fitting a component to make that section of binding gap-free will avoid the need to cover it up before applying a finish by resorting to copious amounts of the dreaded filler. This is rarely successful and can result in an ugly result that will come back to haunt you.

Remember also that by having to overcome a problem, by repairing a crack or replacing a section, you are conjointly perfecting your repair and restoration techniques – invaluable skills if you want to do this as a business.

8. Be Inventive

Don't just take my word for it. If there is a particular operation you find hard or that causes more problems than it is worth, find another solution. When I started out, there were certain parts of the building process that I dreaded. After a while, I realized that these issues were detrimental to progress and to my nerves, so having identified each problem that I was having, I found a solution that worked for me. In that way, I ensured that the whole operation became less stressful and far more rewarding.

9. Abrasive Paper

Keep abrasive paper locked up until the end of the process, unless prompted to use any. It is all too tempting to try to smooth off parts along the way, but this can lead to excessive rounding off on edges, which ultimately not only looks unprofessional and aesthetically wrong but can compromise structural strength. Look at other makers' guitars and you will soon see that, apart from obvious profiling of corners for playing comfort, most edges are crisp and clean.

If you want to clean up spots of glue or level bindings flush with the soundboard/**ribs**, use a very sharp scraper. Apart from the fact that this will give you a much better finish, sanding will create problems such as grinding the dust from darker woods used for bindings into the grain of the paler wood of soundboards, which can be very difficult to clean up and very time consuming.

Sanding smooth internal bracing is perfectly acceptable, but should be done with great care and kept to a minimum.

CHAPTER ONE

MATERIALS AND EQUIPMENT

Tools: The Importance of Quality, Sharpness and Good Technique

Quality

Although it is not necessary to spend a fortune on tools suitable for instrument-making, buying cheap, poor quality equipment is a false economy. It is better to purchase fewer good quality hand tools than many sub-standard ones.

As a general rule, buy the best you can afford. You will probably initially only need three or four sizes of chisels, for example, so buying ones with good quality steel blades is best. You will find that these will require far less sharpening as they will hold an edge for a lot longer. The same is certainly true of plane irons – a source of huge frustration when they are not cutting thin, long shavings but are producing irregular chippings or, worse still, are digging in and tearing out parts of the timber's surface.

Sharpness

If you are at all unsure of your ability to sharpen chisels and plane irons effectively, see the 'Sharpening Procedures' feature in this section. This details a system which has worked well for many years. Once you have perfected a good technique, it should come naturally and this will inspire you to use it regularly.

OPPOSITE PAGE:
Just some of the tools and materials needed for guitar-making.

WHAT IS SHARPNESS?

Generally, a cutting edge is formed by two surfaces meeting at a point. This point has no thickness, for all intents and purposes, and provides the ultimate cutting tool. If this is not achieved and maintained then it ceases to be effective and will cause poor work and huge frustration.

If we look at a typical chisel or plane iron the point is created by the meeting of a flat back and an angled front (the bevel). The angle of the bevel with relation to the back will determine how effective and with what ease the tool is capable of cutting the timber's surface. The greater the angle, the more resistance it presents to the timber but the stronger the cutting edge will be. Conversely, with a lesser angle, the cutting edge offers less resistance but it is not as strong and will require sharpening more often. (Note that although a lower angle will necessitate more sharpening, it is generally deemed acceptable for a better cutting operation.) Most chisels and plane irons come with either a 25-degree or 30-degree bevel already ground on. You will need to experiment with either angle to ascertain the ideal cutting edge for the work you will be asking the tool to do. For very hard woods like rosewood or ebony, a bevel angle of 25-degrees may be more appropriate.

The condition of the surface of the metal is also important. Most blades will retain tool marks, scratches and imperfections from the manufacturing process. These can translate into irregularities at the cutting edge, which in turn will give you a less-than-smooth timber surface. By eradicating all of these marks, it is possible to achieve a superb planed or chiselled finish. Therefore, the more polished the surfaces, the better the results.

SHARPENING PROCEDURES

Straight out of the box, no plane or similar hand tool is ready to work. Quite often, a bit of fettling and setting up is required, but most importantly the blade needs sharpening. For this you will require the following equipment:

- a diamond stone
- a water stone
- a honing guide
- a stone holder/bench hook
- water for lubricating the stones
- a straight edge (an engineer's square is ideal).

The first thing to determine is that the back of the blade is flat. It is important that at least the first 25mm (1in) behind the cutting edge is level and polished. To do this, wet the diamond stone with water and pass the back of the blade up and down the stone's whole length. Hold the blade securely and level so that it has no chance of tilting. Check regularly with the straight edge to ensure that you are flattening the surface and not grinding a new facet onto it. Check also that you are achieving a consistent surface of fine scratches and, most importantly, that this extends right to the tip of the cutting edge.

When you are satisfied that the back of the blade is perfectly flat, polish the same area on a wetted water stone, first on the coarse side and then on the fine side. Regularly check that the blade back is staying flat. An uneven stone surface will grind a similarly uneven surface onto your blade and undo all the hard work to get it flat. You should now have a flat, highly polished surface to the back of your blade, and the good news is that you should only have to do this once.

Now turn your attention to the bevel. This needs to go through a similar process, but obviously at the required angle to the honing stone's surface. This is where a honing guide comes into use. There are many different types but generally they all hold the blade at a consistently correct angle. Set this up as recommended by the manufacturer of the guide for the angle you require and then proceed to hone the bevel on the diamond stone that has been wetted with water. Again, hold the assembly securely but not over-firmly to ensure a positive contact between the blade's bevel and the stone. Keep honing across the whole area of the stone until you have fine scratch marks across the whole bevel, especially to the tip of the cutting edge. In theory you should now have a flat bevel, but check with the straight edge to see if you have it in reality. Now repeat the process on a wetted water stone, first on the coarse side, then on the fine.

If you have ever filed or abraded a piece of metal, you will have noticed that this produces a raised lip or burr. This will happen when you hone both sides of a blade. If you run your finger carefully under the flat back you will notice that honing the bevel has raised a small burr on the back. To get rid of this, while the tool is still set up in the honing guide run the back of the blade a couple of times over the stone, turn over and then run the bevel side over the stone. Repeat flipping the blade until the burr weakens from having been pushed back and forth and finally falls away. At this point, you should have the ultimate edge.

This procedure can take some practice, and won't be perfect every time, but with patience and perseverance it will become easy and second nature.

There are several ways of ascertaining the resulting sharpness of your blade. One way is to do a light test: put the blade under a good light source and, if the surfaces of the blade are flat and polished, the light will be reflected back in a consistent and even fashion. If the surface is not perfectly flat, however, it will be very obvious that it is facetted due to the light being reflected unevenly. This can produce the phenomenon where it looks like there is a line of light (known as a 'candle') along the tip of the blade. If there is any evidence of this, the surface is not flat and needs more work. Another way of testing for sharpness is, of course, to use it – but try on a piece of scrap wood first so you don't spoil your cherished (and often expensive) wood.

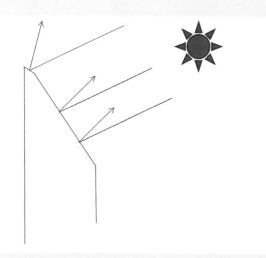

Example of candle on blade.

ADDITIONAL SHARPENING ADVICE

Once you have a truly sharp blade or iron, handle it with care and store it securely so that the edge can't be damaged. If it is a plane iron, don't put the plane down on its sole; leave the plane on its side.

If you are going to plane a piece of timber that is wider than the plane's blade (as with soundboards, **back**s, ribs, and so on) gently round off the very sharp corners of the bevel with a diamond file. It is virtually impossible to set up a blade in a plane perfectly parallel to the sole, and if left sharp one of these corners will invariably dig into the surface of the timber and leave a furrow.

Unlike plane blades, leave the corners of chisel bevels as sharp as possible. This will enable you to cut right into tight corners and angles. Flatten the surface of water stones regularly to maintain the ideal honing surface.

Good Techniques

SETTING UP YOUR PLANE

Once you have a perfectly sharpened plane iron it needs to be set up in the plane body in such a way as to be at its most effective. A mistake a lot of people make is to think that having a large amount of blade protruding from the sole of the plane will enable them to cut large swathes of wood all in one go. This is just not feasible, and if attempted will result in torn timber surfaces, blunt cutting edges and shredded nerves.

The majority of planing work will be to smooth and level the surfaces of the guitar's components and not to remove significant amounts of timber. If you are trimming to a line, remove excess wood with a band-saw and only plane the final 0.5–1mm. If the plane's blade is set to cut very fine shavings you will have far more control over flatness, accuracy and so on.

When assembling the plane, ensure that the capping iron is set back approximately 1mm from the blade's cutting edge. Wind the blade far enough out so that you can see it clearly by looking down the sole from the front. The cutting edge should be perfectly horizontal with the sole of the plane – if it is not, adjust the lateral lever positioned under the frog to achieve this. Wind the blade back into the plane until it just disappears from view.

If you are planing a rough-sawn surface, imagine it as having a series of peaks in the timber. When you first pass the plane over this surface it will only cut off the tips of these peaks and appear not to be planing much away. Don't be tempted to wind out more of the plane's blade but instead persevere with consecutive passes; if the plane is set up correctly it will cut off more each time until whole shavings are cut from the timber's surface. It is much better to cut fine shavings than thick ones, as you will have far more control over the levelling process and the plane will cut in a much easier fashion.

EXAMPLE: CUTTING A DOVETAIL

Mark out the dovetail profile with a hard pencil and, when satisfied with its symmetry and positioning, score around the profile with a sharp marking knife. It is only necessary to cut deep enough to ensure a distinct permanent line.

Cut out the waste with a saw to within 0.5mm of the finished line. Mount the timber securely in a vice and at an appropriate working height. If you are right-handed, push the index finger of your left hand against the work, level with the section to be trimmed, place the chisel's cutting edge lightly against the waste portion to be cut, and place the thumb of your left hand onto the top of the chisel's blade. Ensure your index finger is rolled far enough back to be behind the cutting edge, hold the chisel handle with your right hand and carefully pare off a fine shaving of waste wood. Repeat the shaving steadily lower, until the final cut can be made by locating the cutting edge into the scored line and paring across the cut.

If possible, use a chisel that is wider than the timber you are cutting. If the chisel is narrower the final surface will have to be achieved in more than one cut and therefore will be less likely to be perfectly flat.

It is a common mistake when using a chisel to pare downhill, resulting in the dovetail shoulders sloping inwards. You can avoid this by the following:

- Cut into the dovetail shoulder from the front and from the back, slightly uphill and peaking in the middle.
- Continue until you reach the scored line either side. Make your final cut from the scored line at the side of the shoulder.

SHARPENING SCRAPER BLADES

SQUARE-EDGED SCRAPER BLADES

On a diamond stone, run at least the first 12.7mm (½in) from one long edge of the scraper up and down until it has a consistent covering of fine scratches from the stone. Turn the blade over and repeat on the opposite side. Next upend the blade onto the thin edge and hone it until it is flat and square to the sides. To help keep the blade vertical, place it against a known square piece of wood as you move it over the stone.

Repeat the above on a *flat* waterstone to polish the three faces. As the stone is a lot softer than the diamond, move the scraper's edge around the stone so that you do not create a furrow in the stone's surface. You need to end up with both surfaces adjacent to the thin edge flat and polished, and the edge itself flat, polished, square to the sides and also, very importantly, with very sharp corners between the edge and the sides.

You next want to employ a tool called a 'burnisher'. This is essentially a hardened polished steel rod attached to a handle. It is possible to use other tools for this operation (such as the side of a screwdriver shaft) but they must be made of harder steel than that of the scraper.

Lay the scraper on the flat surface of a bench, with the polished edge flush with the front of the bench. Hold it down with one hand and run the burnisher relatively firmly across the flat face of the scraper, backwards and forwards as if you are stropping the surface. The idea behind this is to draw to the edge a small hook of metal and to work-harden the edge. Now move the scraper so that the first 12.7mm (½in) hangs over the front of the bench. Hold it very firmly with one hand and place the shaft of the burnisher vertically against the scraper's edge. Firmly, but without excessive pressure, drag the burnisher along the scraper's edge from one end to the other. This should displace the hook and turn it up 90 degrees to the flat side of the scraper.

Repeat this operation two or three times, but each time tilt the burnisher a little until the hook is turned to between 85–75 degrees to the flat side of the scraper. Now if you run a finger very carefully across the edge of the scraper you should be able to feel a raised hook.

TAKE CARE

Excessive pressure with the burnisher can tear the hook and create a jagged cutting edge.

BEVEL-EDGED SCRAPER BLADES

Some heavier scraper blades, especially those in scraper planes, have a bevel ground onto one edge, similar to a plane blade. In fact, the bevel must be honed in exactly the same way as for a plane iron or chisel. Flatten and polish the back of the blade, then flatten and polish the bevel until you achieve a good sharp edge. Ensure you also grind off any burr that honing might have thrown up. Run the burnisher relatively firmly across the flat back of the scraper, backwards and forwards as if you are stropping the surface. The idea behind this is to draw to the edge a small hook of metal and to work-harden the edge. Finally rest the burnisher on the bevel, and run it from one end to the other three or four times, each time tilting the burnisher further back to create a hook on the back of the bevel.

USING CHISELS

If you have a very sharp chisel, there is no need to utilize a mallet to aid the cutting process. By hitting the chisel you relinquish any firm control over its cutting action. Better to have a secure grip on the chisel with both hands (obviously behind the cutting edge) and pare across the timber's surface, like a plane, taking off very fine shavings.

USING SCRAPERS

A scraper in its simplest form is a piece of flexible steel. These rudimentary tools are hugely underrated and under used. Because they are not always the easiest tool to set up and sharpen, they are often abandoned in favour of abrasives. However, this would be to miss out on a truly effective weapon in your arsenal of shaping, levelling and smoothing tools. The dangers of over-sanding have already been stated. If a little time and patience are put into preparing scraper blades, then you should find that they will become your first choice when it comes to cleaning up surfaces, levelling bindings flush and for the final shaping of neck heels.

Because scrapers cut rather than abrade, the resultant finish will be far superior to a sanded one. The cutting edge is in fact a burr or hook, which is intentionally raised on the edge of the scraper. However, getting this sharp and at a suitable angle is the key.

As on plane and chisel blades, the more blemish-free and polished the surface, the finer the cut will be. Therefore, the initial preparation on the scraper is very important.

ACHIEVING FLATNESS

To check that the surface of a piece of timber is flat, you need to compare it to a known straight and flat face. The most usual method is to use a good quality straight edge that is long enough to span the whole length of the timber. Hold the wood up to a good light source, rest the straight edge onto the face under test (if the straight edge has a bevel, use this edge) and ascertain if there is any light visible between the straight edge and the timber's surface. It is important to get certain surfaces perfectly flat, so if you can see any light at all then it is not flat and needs more work.

It is necessary to check longitudinal flatness (end to end, parallel to the wood's long sides), width flatness (parallel to the ends) and diagonal flatness (corner to corner). Check at more than one point across the width and length to ensure that there are no lumps and bumps. To determine that you haven't planed a twist to the surface (by allowing the plane to fall off at the end of the pass in one corner – see later section 'Good Planing Technique') it is necessary to lay the straight edge from corner to corner on both diagonals. This will highlight any obvious humps or dips.

When it is necessary to glue together two components, especially if it is a butt joint (not joined mechanically but relying solely on the glue), it is very important to get the two mating surfaces as exact as possible. Any gaps, lumps or irregularities will weaken the joint and result in an ugly glue line. Forcing two irregular surfaces together by excessive clamping pressure will build in unnecessary tension and could well result in the failure of the joint.

If you are having difficulty planing both surfaces flat – for example, the length flatness is fine but the width has a slight arch – try planing across the grain from side to side, or even diagonally, taking off very fine shavings with a very sharp blade. This will create a slightly roughened surface, so finish by going with the grain.

CHECKING FOR SQUARENESS

If asked to plane an adjacent side flat and square it to the **datum face**, the side should first be checked for flatness using the above method and in addition it should be ascertained that the side is at 90 degrees to the datum face. A good quality engineer's square placed at regular intervals along the datum face will tell you if this has been achieved. Again, hold the timber up to a good light source and if any light is visible between the engineer's square and the wood's surface then it is not achieving the desired 90 degrees!

It is very common when planing an edge to have a tendency to lean the plane either to the left or the right of horizontal. The trick is to be aware of when you are doing this and to make a concerted effort to correct it. If the timber you are preparing is not affected by the direction in which you are planing (see next section) then turn the wood around and plane it from the other end until the side is back to the horizontal (90 degrees to the datum face). If planing in one direction is the only option, however, you will need to tip the plane physically to correct the angle.

PLANING

The wood you are preparing must be held in such a way as to avoid it moving whilst you concentrate on planing its surface. If planing a relatively small piece of timber, mounting it in a vice is normally sufficient. If it is a large piece of wood like a neck blank, however, place it on top of the bench and clamp a lower piece of wood onto the bench as an end stop. If you have a proper woodworking bench it may be already equipped with bench stops or 'dogs'. The idea is that the timber is pushed up against the stop and the pressure from the planing will keep it in place. (One big advantage of this set up is that, as the timber is not clamped in place, it is easy to pick it up and check it for flatness and squareness regularly.)

It is very important that the front of the plane can pass over the end of the timber and not be impeded by the end stop or the clamp. The following describes the planing technique if you are right handed; if, like me, you are left handed, simply reverse hands.

Stand at one end of the timber (standing over it will not give you enough downward pressure) at a slight angle and with your legs spread slightly to give you good balance. Lean back on your right hip and start planing whilst slowly shifting your weight to your left knee. (For those who have ever done Tai Chi, you will be very familiar with this move. Do not overstretch, as this will affect your balance.

It is important that the plane starts cutting at the start of the timber, rather than some way in. Place the front of the sole of the plane onto the beginning of the wood, exert some downward pressure on the rear handle and push the plane forward. Try to plane smoothly from one end to the other – small scrubbing motions are counterproductive and result in uneven surfaces. When the plane gets to the far end, do not let it drop over the edge. Envisage a piece of wood longer than the piece you are working on so that you keep going. If you maintain the downward pressure on the back handle, this should reduce the tendency to let the plane drop at the end of each stroke.

If the timber is wider than the plane you are using, skew the plane at an angle whilst still planing in a forward direction. This will help to keep the width of the wood flat. It also helps with ease of planing, especially on wood with an awkward grain or highly figured timbers, as the plane blade is slicing the surface as opposed to cutting all at once in a straight line.

Depending on how the wood has been cut, and the amount of grain runout it has (that is, grain not running parallel to the surface of the timber), it is not unusual to discover that the timber planes better in one direction. If whilst planing the surface you get a lot of grain **tear-out**, turn the piece around and plane from the opposite direction. This invariable cures the problem. If not, it could be due to a particularly awkward section of figuring, in which case a very sharp scraper could be the answer.

Planing the end grain

The ends of planks of wood are often referred to as end grain. Planing these ends smooth and square is not without difficulty as the surface is very hard, but as always the answer is a very sharp and well set-up plane. A block plane is ideal for this, as the blade is set at a low angle and is designed to cope with tough grain. Ensure that the blade is honed as sharp as possible and that it is set to cut extremely fine shavings.

If possible, hold the timber upright in a vice, with only a small amount projecting above the vice jaws. To prevent damage to the longitudinal grain as the plane passes over the far edge of the end grain, place a piece of scrap wood directly behind the main piece, perfectly level with it. Plane right across both pieces, taking very fine shavings, and check regularly that the end is square to the sides.

Planing problems and possible solutions

When checking for longitudinal flatness, if the timber is arched (dips at each end) then you are not planing in a straight and consistent line. Plane a small section in the middle of the timber, gradually working outwards towards the ends, checking regularly that the surface is becoming flat.

If it is difficult to plane an edge square to the datum face you are tipping the plane to one side. Carefully curl your left index finger under the plane (make sure it is nowhere near the blade) and press it against the side of the timber. This will act as a guide and help to pull the plane into a horizontal position.

GLUING

When gluing two surfaces together, it is only necessary to use sufficient glue to wet the surface of the wood. An excess of glue will not make sections stick together better! This has quite the opposite effect, in fact, especially if the surplus glue has nowhere to go. Conversely, too little glue will starve a joint, and it will ultimately fail.

USING ANIMAL GLUE

As this glue has a high water content when mixed and heated, its application will inevitably swell the wood fibres surrounding the joint thus making fitting more difficult. It is good practice to first paint the surfaces of the joint thinly with animal glue to seal the end grain, allowing it to dry thoroughly. This may require a small amount of refitting but on the second application of hot glue there will be less likelihood of the wood fibres expanding.

CLAMPING

When clamping two components together, such as the headstock section to neck blank, the clamping pressure should be spread evenly by utilizing **caul**s (wooden blocks). These will also prevent damage to the component's surfaces from the clamps themselves. To prevent the cauls becoming glued to the joint it is good practice to isolate them with a non-stick barrier, either waxed paper, or, best of all, a Teflon-coated baking sheet. This is ideal, as any dried glue can be simply brushed off and the sheet re-used many times.

PREPARING A TIMBER BLANK

There is a logical way to prepare a piece of timber, which is as follows.

1. Plane Face 'A' flat (*see* 'Achieving Flatness' earlier in this chapter).
2. Plane Face 'B' flat and at 90 degrees to Face 'A' (*see* 'Checking for Squareness' earlier in this chapter).
3. Mark Face 'A' and Face 'B' as datum faces. Set a marking gauge to the required finished width and run the gauge from the Face 'B' datum edge to score around four faces a line denoting the finished width.

USING A MARKING GAUGE

Don't use the marking gauge with the pin at 90 degrees to the surface of the wood. The resultant line can be erratic and over deep. Locate the gauge with the pin lying sideways, roll the gauge until the pin just touches the wood, and score along at this angle. The line will be far more accurate and deep enough to leave a permanent mark.

---

4. If the waste from Face 'C' is excessive, saw off to within 1mm of the line. Plane down to this line and check that new Face 'C' is flat, square to Face 'A' and parallel to face 'B'.
5. Set the marking gauge to the required finished thickness, run the gauge from Face 'A' and score around four faces a line denoting the finished thickness.
6. Again, if the waste from Face 'D' is excessive, saw off to within 1mm of the line. Plane down to this line, and

check that new Face 'D' is flat, square to Face 'B' and parallel to face 'A'.
7. If required, plane Face 'E' and Face 'F'. With an engineer's square and a marking knife, score a line around four faces to denote a good square end for Face 'E'.
8. If there is excessive wood (or the rough-sawn end is very unsquare), saw off the excess to within 0.5mm of the line and plane to the line with a very sharp block plane (*see* 'Planing the End Grain' earlier in the chapter). Check that the new Face 'E' is flat and square to Face 'A' and Face 'B'.
9. Measure precisely the required overall length, score a line around four faces to denote the finished measurement, cut off the excess to within 0.5mm of the line and plane to the line with a very sharp block plane. Check new Face 'F' is flat and square to Face 'A' and Face 'B'.

You should now have a flat, square and parallel piece of timber!

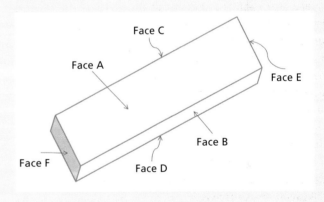

Planing a block to be flat and square.

The Importance of Using Hand Tools Over Machinery

As previously discussed, mass-produced instruments are made to a formula; that is, all components are fabricated in an identical fashion, with the same dimensions and so on. When making a handmade instrument, you want to get the optimum performance from each piece of timber so it is vital that you get to know each item, as they will all have their

own characteristics. Simply putting a soundboard through a planer or sander to produce a pre-conceived thickness misses the point. By contrast, hand-planing small amounts off the wood's surface and constantly checking the flexibility and tone helps to ensure that a particular piece of timber is allowed to work at its best. I am also a firm believer that this way you gain a much better understanding of how this all works – I call it the Zen of guitar-making.

Health and Safety

A vast amount of health and safety considerations are based on common sense, but it is worth emphasizing a few salient points.

Dust hazard   Some woods traditionally used in luthiery can produce dust that is an irritant. There are makers who choose not to use certain timbers like rosewood, as handling these woods can produce side effects such as skin rashes. Although this is relatively rare, it is well worth taking into consideration when making your choice of materials. When cutting the wood, even if it is a softwood like spruce, err on the side of caution and wear a mask. Use extraction functions on all machinery for your sake and also to keep your work area as dust-free as possible. However innocuous it may seem, the less dust you breathe into your lungs the better!

Sharpness   Whilst impressing on you the importance of getting tools like plane blades and chisels as sharp as you possibly can, always bear in mind the implications of one careless slip if you are not holding the tool properly (that is, with both hands behind the cutting edge). If you attempt to use a tool that is less than sharp, it will require far more pressure to pass its cutting edge through the timber's surface. This results in excessive force being used, and is far more likely to lead to tools slipping and harming the handler. Conversely, if a truly sharp tool is utilized, its cutting edge will pare through the wood with far greater ease and therefore less pressure, resulting in better control and far safer handling.

Cutting edges   When using any machinery, especially bandsaws and routers, consider how close your hands are to the cutting blade. It is well worth taking ten minutes to make a jig to hold and guide your work. This will aid the safety of the cutting operation, with less risk of harming yourself. If you are a player, the last thing you want is cut and sore hands – try playing the thinnest steel string on your guitar with a cut across your fingertip and you will get the point.

Safety guards   Guards on machinery are put there to prevent your fingers being too close to cutting edges. Although they can sometimes be deemed an annoyance, discard them at your peril!

Workspace   Keep work areas clean and clear of unnecessary tools, timber and equipment. Working amongst clutter is bad practice and can lead to poor work or damage to the work (a carelessly discarded screw or sharp object can seriously indent soundboard material, often with no real possibility of rectification, for example).

How you feel   Don't work when tired or distracted. This is when very little will be achieved and there is a strong possibility that you could undo hours of good work because you are not concentrating. Guitar-making should be enjoyable, so if you are not in the mood or fully committed leave it for another time.

Essential Tools

I remember reading once someone claimed that they could make a musical instrument on the kitchen table with a knife and fork. This is a bit of a simplification to say the least, and while it is true you don't need hundreds of tools to make a guitar, the list below itemizes some of the necessary tools used to make the guitar detailed here.

Chisels   A set from ¼in to 1in.

Gouges   Arguably not essential, but very useful for those tricky corners.

Inlay trench 'pickers'   Thin, shaped chisels for excavating narrow channels.

A bradawl   For indenting hole centres.

Saws   **Fret** slot cutting saws, various Japanese and razor saws, and hacksaws.

Measuring tools   6in and 12in rules, straight edges, vernier gauges, engineers squares and sliding bevels.

Files   Various hand cut files, rasps, needle files, and a Japanese saw file.

Knives   A craft knife, a carving knife, a scalpel and various blades.

Scrapers   Of various sizes, shapes and thickness.

A *burnisher* For turning a hook on the scraper blades.

Planes A no.4 smoothing plane, block and scraper planes, and thumb and palm planes.

Spokeshaves Flat and curved base, and miniature for awkward places.

Clamps Wooden cam, various size spring clamps, F- and G-clamps. (You can never have too many clamps!)

Lightweight routers A minitool (for example, a **Dremel** for light work like **soundhole** inlays).

Heavy-duty routers Powerful ones will be needed for routing **truss rod** slots and so on.

Drills Hand and electric.

Drill bits Micro drills, Forstner bits, twist drills.

Sharpening stones Water stones and diamond stones.

Honing guides For consistent and accurate sharpening.

Hammers Pin hammers and deadblow hammers.

A *purfling marker* To score position of bindings.

Reamers For tapered holes, such as those for **bridge pin**s.

Specialist luthier tools

An *electric bending iron* A heated casting for bending the ribs/sides.

A *bending strap* A flexible metal strap with handles used to aid the bending process.

Chisels, gouges and various workshop-made inlay pickers.

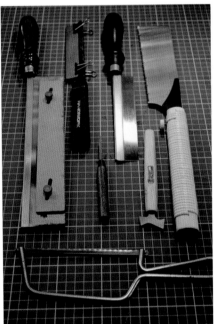

Various fret slot saws, a razor saw, a Japanese saw, a junior hacksaw and a bridge pin slotting saw.

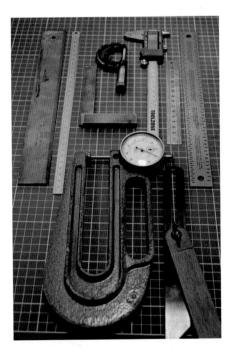

A straight edge, rules, a vernier gauge and micrometer, a string spacing rule, thickness calipers, a sliding bevel and engineer's square.

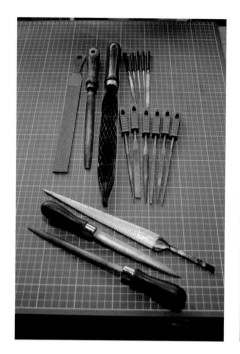

Various hand-cut files, a Japanese saw file and diamond needle files.

A Stanley knife, burnisher, various scraper blades, a scalpel and blades, a carving knife.

Smoothing planes, block plane, scraper plane, thumb plane, palm plane and spokeshaves.

A wooden cam clamp, spring clamps, bridge clamp, hobby clamp, F-clamp and G-clamps.

A Dremel minitool and accessories, micro drills, a battery hand drill, Forstner and twist drills.

A water stone, diamond stone, various honing guides, bench hook with plate glass and wet-and-dry abrasive for flattening water stones.

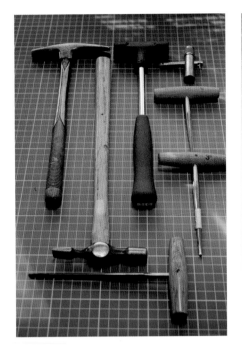

Pin hammers, a deadblow hammer, a purfling marker, reamers

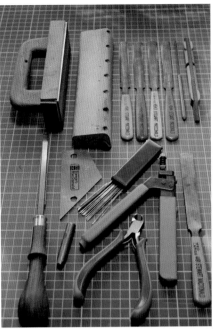

A fret leveller, fret end chamfer file, nut files, fret end manicure file, sanding stick, fret reprofiling file, fret tang cutter, fret end nippers, welder's nozzle cleaners, brass fret seating tool, fret rocker and fret reprofiling file.

An electric bending iron and bending strap.

Machinery

As with tools it is not necessarily essential that you own much in the way of machinery, but at least having access to some of the following will greatly aid your work. This equipment will save a lot of time by being able to do mundane tasks like converting large planks of wood to more manageable pieces, leaving you with more time to concentrate on the instrument-making.

View of workshop: showing a floor-standing bandsaw, dust extractor, bobbin sander and anglepoise lamps with daylight bulbs.

Bandsaws A floor-standing bandsaw is good for converting large pieces to more manageable sizes relatively accurately. A tabletop version is better for finer work, especially cutting out soundboards and backs.

A drill press For accurate drilling of components.

A bobbin sander This is very useful for finishing curved components like a mould.

View of workshop: showing a tabletop bandsaw, drill press, storage drawers and under-bench shelves for storing soundboards backs and neck blanks.

View of workshop: showing work board clamped to the bench, storage drawers and chisel racks.

Materials

Woods Traditionally Used

There is a strong tradition of using certain woods for guitar-making, and many makers insist that this is as true today as it has ever been. Many luthiers insist that Brazilian rosewood is the only truly superior tonewood for backs and sides. Unfortunately, this wood is now so rare that there is a worldwide ban on its export and usage. Only old stock that is certified as such can be used legitimately to make guitars. Adirondack spruce was so over-logged that usable sizes have also been unavailable for some time. It is just making a tentative comeback, but in small quantities. Some true mahogany species are disappearing, and Indian rosewood, ebony and other exotic hardwoods are becoming more and more expensive as good quality examples are increasingly difficult to find.

The musical instrument industry has a dilemma, as a lot of woods traditionally used in guitar-making are now becoming scarce. Consequently, makers have a moral obligation to find alternatives.

Alternative Woods and Materials

You will probably hear the word 'tradition' used a lot when it comes to musical instruments. To some more progressive, modern makers it is a dirty word, but to others it is what instrument making is all about. What these people mean when they say that guitars have been 'traditionally' made with certain woods is that generations of luthiers found those woods to make the best-sounding instruments – so why change a tried-and-trusted formula? This argument would hold true if we had access to an unlimited source of these timbers but, as previously stated, this is no longer the case. A lot of luthiers, and even large manufacturers like Martin and Gibson, are using alternative woods and materials, and with very impressive results.

Glues

It is very important to choose the right glue for instrument-making. It has to be strong to withstand the considerable stress some of the joints will be put under, but consideration should also be given to the fact that some components may have to be disassembled during the guitar's lifetime for repair or replacement. For this reason, glues such as two-part epoxies should be avoided in the general construction process.

Historically, the glue used for instrument-making was animal glue. Although this is still used by makers today, the steel string industry made a big move to synthetic glues. Interestingly, lately there has been a return by some to animal glue, as people have experimented with how different glues affect tone and vibration transfer from one component to another. The following will hopefully help you to make an informed choice.

ANIMAL GLUE

This is often supplied in granular or flake form and needs to be added to water and heated until it achieves the correct consistency. Once the glue is applied, and it starts to cool, it will harden very quickly. (*See* 'Animal Glue Mixing Method' later in this chapter for tips on how to prepare it.)

Reversibility

Advantage – One of the big benefits of animal glue is that its action is easily reversible. A joint with animal glue, even one that was constructed many years before, can be parted by using either heat or dampness. This is an obvious advantage in that instruments constructed with this type of glue can be taken apart and repaired or reset as needed. The old glue can even be re-flowed to close the joint.

Disadvantage – This property could render an instrument's joints susceptible to coming apart in extremes of heat or humidity. Having said that, however, would you want to keep a valuable instrument in these sorts of conditions?

Set time

Advantage – Animal glue sets very quickly. As a result it can be used on joints that are very awkward to clamp, so they can be held together by hand for just a minute (as with the 'v' joint on some guitar neck headstocks), or if you want to temporarily spot-glue two components together quickly.

Disadvantage – A fast set time can be seen as a major drawback as you have a very short 'open time' in which to glue components together. For a large area (such as the soundboard to ribs) you would normally have to dry clamp the whole structure, remove two or three clamps at a time and feed sufficient glue into the joint, re-clamp and then repeat with the next two or three clamps. Hot animal glue sets very quickly as it cools and the water content evaporates, so often the only way it can be successfully applied is by having the workshop very warm, and even by gently heating the wood of each part. This goes some way to stopping the glue solidifying too quickly, but these conditions are not always possible to achieve.

Strength

Advantage – Animal glue is very strong. If mixed correctly and applied in the right quantity, it can withstand the extreme tensions exerted on guitar joints.

Disadvantage – Its sheer strength can fail if put under excessive stress, although it can be argued that this does have its merits. For example, if a guitar **bridge** is glued on with animal glue and excessively high string tension is exerted on it, the joint can break. The good news, however, is that the bridge will invariably come off quite cleanly and therefore will not be difficult to repair. (If it had not parted company with the soundboard, the over-tensioned strings could have caused far more damage by distorting or even cracking the guitar's top.)

Readiness

Disadvantage – As animal glue has to be mixed and heated, it is not available instantly. You usually have to plan the work and decide how much glue you will need for that day's needs. Although animal glue can be reheated for future use, it does tend to lose its strength. Therefore, it is best to mix a fresh batch each time it is required. You can buy bottled hide glue from the American manufacturer Franklin, but as it has an additive to keep it in liquid form it is generally considered to have inadequate strength for the vast majority of guitar work. It also has a very short shelf-life.

Cost

Advantage – This type of glue is relatively cheap, as it is a by-product of the meat industry.

Disadvantage – You may have moral problem with using this type of glue due to its source.

Solidity/hardness

Advantage – One of the reasons some makers are going back to using animal glue is that it cures to a very hard state. This, it is argued, better transfers tone and vibration from one of the guitar's components to another.

Animal glue mixing method

For guitar-making you would usually add the same amount of water as glue (that is, a 1:1 ratio). Although heated glue pots are readily available, the simplest method is to put sufficient dry glue into a clean screwtop jar, top up with an equal amount of water and allow the mix to soak for approximately half an hour. Put into a saucepan with sufficient water to come to the same level as the glue. Heat gently on a heating ring until the glue starts to liquefy. Eventually the glue will obtain a consistent texture and colour, and should flow off a brush like runny honey. If it clumps or clings to the brush then it is necessary to add more water to the glue mix. If it runs off the brush like water it will be too thin and more dry glue needs to be added.

ACHIEVING THE RIGHT CONSISTENCY

Whilst heating, place the lid loosely on top of the jar but don't screw it on. This will prevent the glue from forming a skin on top. Don't allow the water in the saucepan to fall below the level of the glue in the jar.
Top up if necessary.

SYNTHETIC GLUES

The most commonly used synthetic glue used in guitar-making is a yellow glue known as an aliphatic glue. This was developed to overcome the shortcomings of PVA white glues, namely that they never cure fully hard and they have a tendency to 'creep' under load. This, as you can imagine, is a most undesirable trait, especially on a guitar bridge where the strings are doing their best to pull off the soundboard as it is. White PVA is therefore not recommended for guitar-making!

The aliphatic glue of choice is made by the American company Franklin and is known as Titebond®. There are several versions but the most commonly employed is their Original range, which can be used for the majority of a steel-string guitar's construction. Recently, however, a new version has been introduced called Extend, which has a longer open time and was used on the guitars made in this book for gluing the soundboard and back to the ribs, with good results. A further type of aliphatic glue was also used on the guitars here to construct one type of soundhole inlay. This is a thinner version ideal for this purpose, made by Deluxe Materials™ and called Super 'Phatic.

Some aliphatic yellow glues.

GOOD PRACTICE ADVICE: GLUING

- Always glue freshly planed wood. Dirty or greasy surfaces will not glue well.
- Ensure that the mating surfaces of a joint are as good a fit as possible. Do not rely on the glue to fill a gap – this will lead to a weak joint that could ultimately fail.
- Always do a dry run – this way joints can be checked for gaps and you can ensure that clamps, cauls and non-stick papers will be ready for quick and efficient assembly with glue.
- Only use as much glue as needed to wet the wood's surface. Too much will result in excessive glue squeezing out; too little will give you a starved, weak joint.
- Pre-empt any slippage once the glue is applied and the joint is assembled; make a jig with end stops if applicable.
- Be aware of any distortion or movement to a joint once clamps are applied; consider a **rub joint** if necessary.
- Get into the habit of leaving a freshly glued joint clamped overnight. Always have other work to be getting on with. If gluing and clamping a piece of work means that you cannot work on it until the glue has cured sufficiently, it may be best to make this the last job of the day.
- If in any doubt, try the chosen glue on a test piece to ascertain whether it is suitable for the job required of it.

Reversibility

Disadvantage – Aliphatic glue is far more difficult to reverse than animal glue, as it requires a greater intensity of heat to unglue the joint. This makes it much more likely that the wood, finish and fragile components will be damaged when attempting to take the joint apart (although with adequate protective precautions in place it is still possible).

Set time

Advantage – Synthetic glue takes longer to set and cure than animal glue, thus giving you a longer assembly time.
Disadvantage – Components have to be held together whilst the glue sets. This can be a problem with awkward joints that are difficult to clamp. Once glued, a joint has to be left a lot longer to cure sufficiently.

Strength

Advantage – Aliphatic yellow glue is very strong and it can withstand the extreme tensions exerted on guitar joints.

Disadvantage – This type of glue is generally stronger than the wood that surrounds it. If a guitar bridge is glued on with aliphatic glue, for example, and excessively high string tension is exerted on it which causes the joint to break, the bridge will invariably come off and take a fair portion of the soundboard with it. This can make the instrument difficult to restore, as the soundboard has to be extensively repaired and strengthened before the bridge can be glued back on.

Readiness

Advantage – This type of glue comes straight out of a bottle, so is available instantly.

Cost

Advantage – It is relatively inexpensive.

Solidity/hardness

Advantage – Aliphatic glues cure reasonably hard.

Disadvantage – It is argued that aliphatic glue is not as hard as animal glue when cured (note the earlier comment about tone and vibration transfer).

Luthier Supplies

Although there is a preference for **quarter-sawn** wood to be used in guitar-making, where the direction of the end grain runs at 90 degrees to the surface of the wood, what is equally important is that the timber you use is mature and sufficiently air or kiln dried. The amount of moisture content left in the wood can make all the difference to the stability and integrity of the guitar's structure. Most luthier suppliers won't have the facilities or indeed can afford to store cut timber for years, or even months on end. Consequently, it is possible to buy supplies from some that may be fairly freshly cut. The water content from this timber can be measured with a moisture meter, but you can quite often tell by just handling it.

TAKE CARE

Some woods may not be ready to use.

If the wood you have bought feels anything but bone dry, the chances are it has too much water in it. If you have the time, and if the timber is a particularly good example and ideal for your requirements, it will be worth storing for future making. If, however, you require this wood straight away, you will need to source timber that is ready for use. For this reason, it is preferable to visit the supplier and ask whether you can select your own wood. In this way you can get a better idea of how dry it is, with the added advantage of checking grain orientation, stiffness, figure, and so on.

A professional maker will buy multiple sets of timber so that they can be kept in the workshop for future use. Timber requires careful storage at a suitable temperature and humidity, in such a way as to minimize warping and splitting.

STORAGE OF WOOD

Any timber bought for guitar-making, even wood that is deemed dry and stable, should be stored and allowed to acclimatize to the workshop conditions for several weeks before use. Thin, flat pieces of timber such as soundboard halves, backs and ribs should ideally be stacked on a flat surface, with three or four narrow slats of wood between each piece to allow a flow of air above and below. A weight at each end of the top piece will ensure minimal movement from any of the pieces.

Wood intended for future-making can be left in this way for the duration, although it is a good idea occasionally to go through the stack and check on the condition of each piece, possibly turning them over and determining whether any have taken on a twist or warp. If a component is anything less than flat, it is debatable as to whether it should be used.

Working Conditions

Humidity

To protect your supplies, ideally the workshop should not have wildly fluctuating temperature extremes, or a high level of humidity (moisture content in the atmosphere). Wood is hygroscopic, which means that it will absorb or give off water in balance with the surrounding atmosphere. If the humidity is high, the wood will swell and expand noticeably. Conversely, if the humidity is very low, the wood will shrink. If you construct a guitar while the wood is at either of these extremes then when it is moved to experience dramatically different conditions the wood will either contract, with the danger that it will split or pull open a joint, or it will swell and buckle, upsetting a carefully set-up instrument. When the sound box of the guitar is fully constructed – with the binding glued on and sealing the end grain, the finish applied and sealing the wood pores – it is a relatively stable construction, but it is important that all the components are constructed under moderate humidity conditions. A measurement of around 45–50 per cent humidity is ideal. Any extreme either way should be rectified before you consider gluing any of the components together.

If your workshop has high humidity levels (the most common problem in many workshops), installing a dehumidifier will usually allow you to control the moisture content of the air. Unless you are lucky enough to have a very large working area, a domestic machine is usually sufficient to cope with the average workshop space. Remember to check and

My little helper! Yoda giving timely advice – 'Clean up this bench!'

empty the water tank regularly as these machines can draw an alarming amount of water from the air.

If, however, you have the opposite problem (very low humidity), you need to install some sort of humidifier. This can vary from a water container hung on a radiator to a machine that sprays a fine mist of water vapour into the air at regular intervals.

Heat and humidity are inextricably linked, and one will always affect the other, so if you have heating in the workshop and the air is very dry, consider reducing the heat to a sensible minimum.

Adequate Storage Space

Large tools like planes can be stored in cupboards under benches, carefully placed so that sharp blades cannot be damaged.

View of workshop: showing under-bench storage for planes, components and jigs.

Light tunnel in my workshop roof. I sometimes think I've left the light on!

Lighting

Natural daylight is always preferable to work by, so if possible site your main work area by a window or directly under a skylight. If electric light is required, install daylight bulbs in all fitments. In this way, you will readily see inadequately finished wood surfaces and it will inspire you to try to get the best finish possible. Anglepoise lamps that can be pulled down over a piece of work are also extremely useful.

TAKE CARE

Dust off the tops of your angelpoise lamps regularly. I once pulled one down over a newly varnished instrument to inspect the finish, to be rewarded by a cloud of dust descending onto the still-tacky surface!

Jigs and Moulds

Jigs

Time invested in the making of jigs to aid the building process is time well spent. Not only does it go a long way to ensuring that the operation will be more precise and successful, but you then have a set of jigs that can be utilized again and again for future instruments. Even for a one-off operation, making a jig should never be considered a waste of time.

Jigs can also, as stated previously in the Health and Safety section, ensure you against dangerous practice, like passing too small a piece of wood through a bandsaw with the result that your hands come too close to the blade.

Templates

As with jigs, templates are worth all the time put into making them. It is recommended that three main templates are made for each model of instrument you make – a body outline template, a headstock profile template and the side view of the neck template.

Templates can be made from any stable thin material such as card, but for longevity it is recommended that you use acetate or a thin ply material known as Aeroply™. In addition, it is recommended that templates are made for the back of the neck profile, the rib back curve (acetate) and the bridge plan (if it is an awkward shape).

Using Figured Woods

Highly figured and decorative woods are much sought after in instrument-making circles, especially fiddle-back maple. Figuring (distinct lines or patches that cut across the surface of the wood) occurs in areas where the grain suddenly changes direction and comes to the surface. Although the effect can be quite stunning and add a significant 'bling factor' to the look of an instrument, it can also be argued that this is an imperfection in the wood. The distinctive spots and rings on birdseye maple are actually the result of an insect infestation, for example. Consequently, the planing and bending of such timbers is usually fraught with difficulty. It is not unusual to get tear-out, even whilst using a very sharp plane set for fine shavings. If this happens the best solution is to revert to a scraper, one that has been freshly honed and with a new keen hook turned (*see* 'Tools' at the beginning of this chapter). The bending of such woods has to be done with great caution, as the areas of figure are very vulnerable to cracking; they can be quite unstable and give a rippled surface across the bent rib.

All of this may be deemed worth the trouble due to the end results, but generally the more plain and straight-grained the wood, the easier it is to work. If you are inexperienced at guitar-making it is highly recommended that you start off using good quality but largely un-figured timbers, to enable you to concentrate on perfecting the planing, bending and finishing of guitar components. Your finished product won't sound any the worse for it, and also you will not have to suffer the pain and frustration of ruining what are generally very much more expensive woods (there is always a premium to pay on highly figured timbers).

The mahogany used on Guitar #1 is beautifully figured, but working with it proved to be very troublesome. Thicknessing and preparation could only be achieved by using a scraper plane, and only then if the scraper was skewed at a certain angle to the fiddle-back-type figure. More than one crack started to appear whilst bending, but these were quickly re-glued and strengthened with a brown paper patch. The cutaway was a very tight curve so the piece was thicknessed to 1.5mm (¹⁄₁₆in), bent quite damp by use of a bending strap (a flexible steel sheet with handles at each end) and pulled carefully into shape. (For more on these techniques *see* 'Bending the Ribs' in Chapter 3.)

CHAPTER TWO

THE ANATOMY OF THE STEEL-STRING GUITAR

A Bit of History

The steel-string guitar is primarily the product of American factories, not small-scale individual luthiers. Its very construction points to a design that lends itself to mass production. It has a separate neck and body that is usually only put together at the final stages of the build. The fingerboard invariably stops short of the soundhole, making it easier to produce as the end does not have to be shaped precisely to the soundhole perimeter (as on classical guitars). Commonly it has a flattened top bout that makes shaping the back of the neck heel into a concave profile unnecessary.

Prior to the American Civil War, musical instruments were primarily imported from Europe. However, the subsequent large influx of immigrants coming to the United States brought many who were skilled in instrument-making. As the quality of life improved in the latter half of the nineteenth century, more and more people found time for leisure activities such as music-making. The popularity of banjos, mandolins and guitars grew to such an extent that many companies were established to meet the demand. Large music stores like Lyon and Healy began to make instruments under the name of Washburn, which became hugely successful, and along with companies such as Gibson and Martin have over the years become associated with the development of the steel-string guitar. Many decades later they are still making similarly designed instruments, which are as popular as ever.

In the late 1840s, C.F. Martin Sr started using an **X-brace** system for the guitars he was building. Previous to that, soundboards had been ladder braced (with struts running

horizontally across the guitar) or had a **fan brace** (a system of **brace**s where five to seven thin low-profile braces radiate or fan back from the soundhole and under the bridge). The X-brace was a design innovation that suited the guitars that were being built at that time, but they were still gut-strung instruments and the X-bracing design of the time was relatively lightweight.

It is argued that it was probably the Larson brothers, Carl and August, who, from the end of the nineteenth century and into the twentieth, took the X-brace design and modified it and reinforced it to be able to resist the considerably increased tension of steel strings. They developed laminated braces with either a layer of rosewood or ebony between outer layers of spruce. Their necks were a five-piece ply, with a wedge-shaped core as reinforcement. By the 1930s the brothers had developed a rod system that ran through the guitar from the **neck block** and out through the tail to an adjuster that could be tightened or loosened to adjust the neck angle. They also patented a design for adjusting the height of the bridge. However, they didn't seem to want to grow their business any bigger than the two of them, and never produced on a large scale. They did make for other brands – Maurer, Stahl and Euphonen – and eventually created a range known as Prairie State that featured many of their innovations, but they never put their own names to their creations, which could be the reason for their eventual obscurity.

It was not until the 1920s that companies like Martin started to introduce guitars that offered the option of steel strings. The Larson brothers had, until recently, been all but forgotten, but it is Martin that most makers refer to when quoting their influences. Their soundboard bracing layout has been copied by many builders, mainly because it works so well. It has been tweaked and perfected minutely, but essentially it is the same original design.

OPPOSITE PAGE:
Guitar #1: Left-handed, complete with cutaway and bound fingerboard.

The guitars shown in this book are based on versions of the Martin 000 twelve-fret guitar. Because it is such a proven design, it is a very good place to start. In fact, if made to the drawings available, it would make a very impressive instrument. It is recommended that while you are learning the art of guitar-making you stick with a proven design. Once you are confident that you have mastered the intricacies of building an instrument that is structurally sound and performs well, then experiment with bracing, soundboard thicknesses and so on. When you are starting out the important thing is not necessarily what you make, it is how you make it. Leave that treble neck, fan-fretted resonator as a project for the future!

Primary Components of a Steel-String Guitar's Soundboard

This has a number of braces and struts glued across its internal face. Some give the soundboard its structural integrity, whilst others are placed to influence the soundboard's tone.

Fingerboard patch   This light but strong patch is glued across the soundboard join at the top section of the soundboard, under the fingerboard extension area. This is for insurance against the soundboard splitting either side of the fingerboard due to constant flexing of the neck over time.

Transverse brace   This is a substantial brace that is glued across the top half of the soundboard above the soundhole, which defines a border between the mostly resonant lower half of the soundboard and the largely non-resonant top section where the fingerboard extension and neck join reside.

Soundhole braces   The soundhole is a relatively large aperture to have in the middle of the upper half of the soundboard, and without any extra support this area would be vulnerable to caving in due to bridge torque and string pressure. A lot of designs show thin patches of a thickness similar to the front, but, as this is considered not substantial enough, taller but narrower braces are employed on the guitars featured here.

X-Brace   This is mainly structural, as it forms the major support for the soundboard and is made up of two separate arms that are joined at their intersection to form an 'X' shape. However, depending on its shaping and rigidity it will affect the sound given by the soundboard.

Finger braces   These are fairly light braces that radiate out from the lower legs of the X-brace. They are considered to be **tone bars**, but they also are structural in the same way as the soundhole braces in that they resist the possibility of the area caving in due to bridge torque and string pressure.

Tone bars   These radiate out from the treble side lower arm of the X-brace and are the only asymmetrical components on the soundboard – that is, the rest of the bracing is symmetrical (a mirror image either side of the centre line). For a left-handed version they should radiate from the other lower arm of the X-brace. These bars are placed to balance the response of the soundboard; as the treble strings have more tension than the bass strings, the treble side of the soundboard requires more structural integrity.

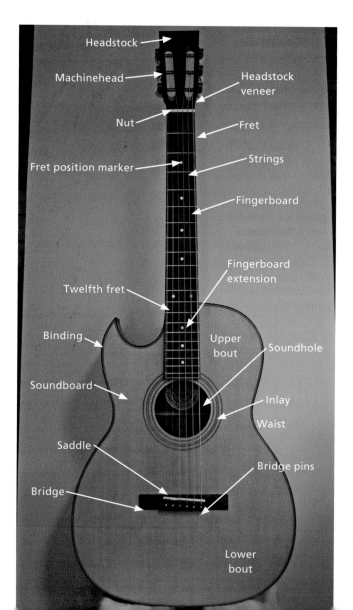

The anatomy of the guitar.

The anatomy of the soundboard.

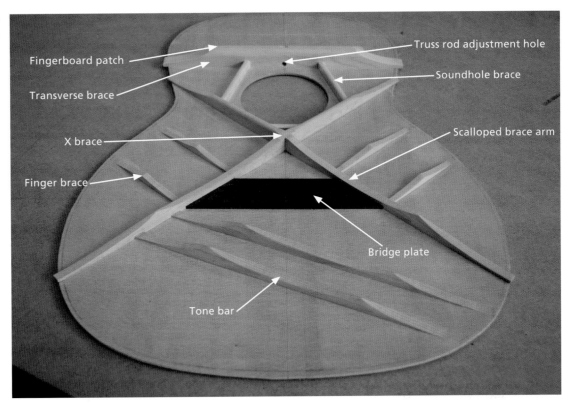

Fingerboard patch

Truss rod adjustment hole

Transverse brace

Soundhole brace

X brace

Scalloped brace arm

Finger brace

Bridge plate

Tone bar

The anatomy of the guitar back.

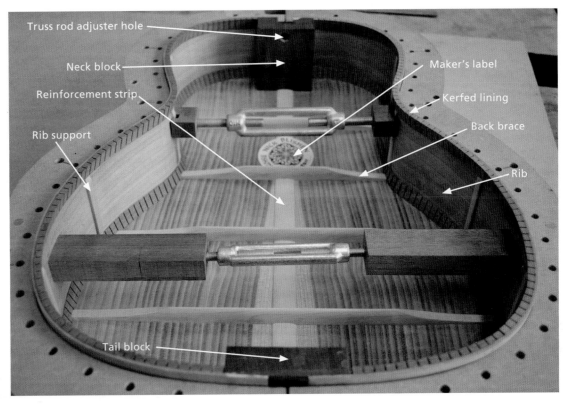

Truss rod adjuster hole

Neck block

Maker's label

Reinforcement strip

Kerfed lining

Back brace

Rib support

Rib

Tail block

37

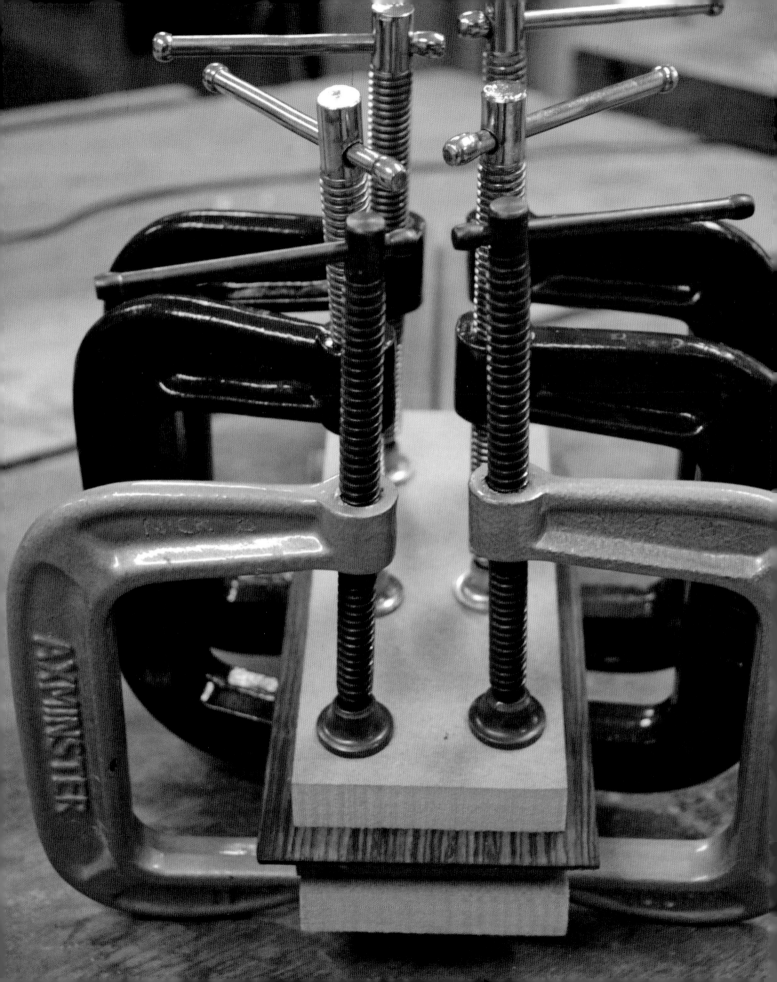

CHAPTER THREE

MAKING THE COMPONENT PARTS

Making the Primary Templates

Materials required

- The instrument plan;
- stable thin material (card, acetate or aeroply);
- tracing paper;
- a hard pencil (2H);
- a soft pencil (HB);
- an indelible pen.

The Body Outline Template

The body outline template is an important one to get right. Not only is it used to determine the outline of the mould, but it is used to mark out the soundboard and the back and their relevant **brace** positions, the soundhole centre, and so on. It is well worth taking time to get the outline curves as smooth and as accurate to the body shape as possible.

First, lay out the plan drawing and ensure the body shape is in full view and resting on a supportive surface. If the outline is symmetrical (the left and right halves are identical) then you only require a half template.

Draw a long straight line towards one edge of the tracing paper and lay this over the centre line of the body profile. Use weights to hold the tracing paper in place (tape will invariably damage the surface of the plan) and carefully and precisely trace the outline with a hard pencil (a soft pencil will give you an indistinct line).

Turn the tracing paper over and scribble with the soft pencil around the whole profile line.

Ensure that one long edge of the aeroply is dead straight and flat and turn the tracing paper back over and tape or weight it onto the template material (ensuring that the straight line on the tracing paper is positioned precisely along the straight edge of the ply). Go round the traced profile once again with a hard pencil, pressing reasonably firmly and keeping to the line as best as possible. The graphite from the scribbled soft pencil will transfer the body contours to the template material.

Cut out the template, close to but not crossing the line, and then trim accurately to the line with a sharp knife, a small fine file or sanding blocks. Lay the template over the plan drawing often to ensure that the template profile is following the original shape as accurately as possible.

Once you are satisfied that the template is as good as you can get it, drill a hole in one corner (this will enable you to hang it up with the other templates) and mark on it the model type with an indelible pen. Lay the template back onto the plan and mark on it the relevant positions of the braces, the soundhole centre and so on. To avoid confusion it is a good idea to flip the template over and mark the back braces on the reverse side.

The Headstock Profile Template

Draw directly onto the template material the exact outline of the headstock, along with any hole centres. Cut out precisely to the line.

OPPOSITE PAGE:
The headstock veneer being glued on.

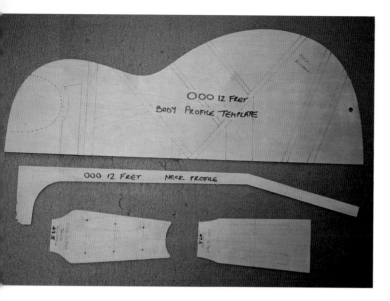

The main templates to be made: a half body template, neck side view and headstock.

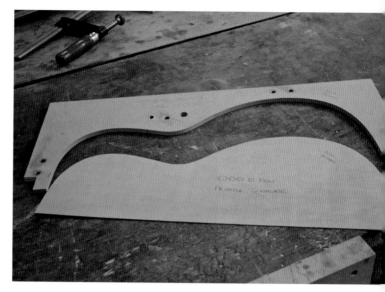

The mould router template with the half body template.

The Neck Side Profile Template

Draw directly onto the template material the exact side view of the neck, which will include the headstock, neck stem and heel profile. Cut out precisely to the line and indicate exactly where the neck joins the body.

The Router Template

A further template can be made to ease the making of the mould. This will be used to guide a router to cut the MDF pieces to an accurate shape.

Materials required
- MDF: 600mm (23⅜in) (L) × 230mm (9¹⁄₁₆in) (W) × 18mm (⁷⁄₁₀in) (T) (1 off);
- M8 nuts (8 off);
- 8mm dowel (1 off);
- a hard pencil (2H).

Lay the body outline template onto the MDF, ensuring the long straight edges of both pieces are aligned. Secure them together using a couple of spring clamps and draw around the outline. Cut the MDF profile on a band-saw to within 1mm of the line. Trim accurately to the line with a bobbin sander, files or sanding blocks.

TAKE CARE

Remember, when cutting or sanding MDF always wear a mask and use adequate extraction on all machinery.

The mould router template: transferring the body shape to MDF pieces.

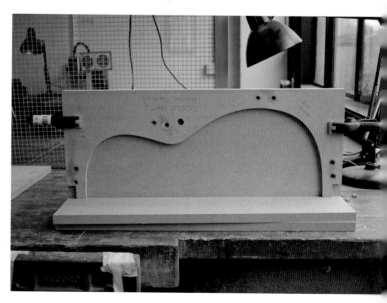

Drill out the middle thread of each M8 nut with an 8mm drill, preferably on a drill press, with the nut held securely in a drill vice. Drill 8mm paired holes at equal intervals around the template's profile. Push the 8mm dowel into one of the M8 nuts, such that a few mm protrude from the bottom of the nut. Locate one of these in each one of the drilled holes, and draw on the outline of the nut. Re-drill all paired holes, this time with a 12.5mm drill bit. Next, with a very sharp ¼in chisel, carefully pare down the sides of the holes up to the drawn-on flats of the nut. Locate a nut in each hole as you go to ensure that you haven't trimmed back too far. You are looking for an interference fit (to use an engineering term), so that the nut sits tightly into the now hexagonal hole.

Ideally it should be only necessary to tap the nut home with a small hammer. If there is any play or movement then remove the nut, smear a small amount of Araldite® or similar glue onto the nut's flats, re-insert it into the hole and allow it to dry. These captivated nuts will now allow you to drill through the template with an 8mm drill into the mould sections many times over without damaging or enlarging the hole positions and they will allow precise repeated placement.

Making the Mould

Cutting the Mould Sections

Material required
- MDF: 600mm (23⅝in) *(L)* × 230mm (9¹⁄₁₆in) *(W)* × 18mm (⁷⁄₁₀in) *(T)* (8 off).

Stand one of the mould sections on its long edge on a flat surface, offer up the router template so that it too sits on the flat surface, and secure the two together using a couple of strong spring clamps.

Draw around the router template, transferring the body outline and the cut-out at each end. With the template still clamped securely to the mould section, use an 8mm drill bit to drill through the mould section through each of the eight captive nuts.

Repeat on the rest of the mould sections. Cut out the body profile on each one on a band-saw to within 1mm of the line.

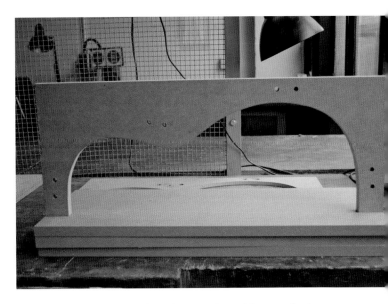

The mould MDF piece (rough cut and awaiting routing).

Routing the Mould Sections

Relocate the router template onto one of the mould sections using four 8mm dowels. Using a flush-cut router set up in a router table, trim off the last 1mm to achieve a very smooth and accurately curved outline.

Repeat this process with the remaining sections.

The mould MDF piece being routed to the exact profile.

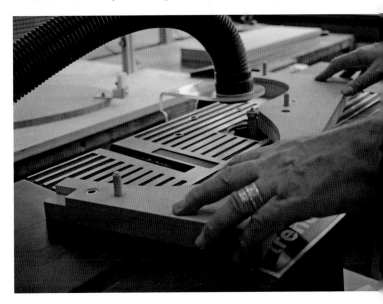

Gluing up the Mould Sections

Materials required

- Newspaper;
- the profiled mould sections (8 off);
- 8mm dowels (24 off);
- Titebond or PVA glue;
- large G-clamps (12 off);
- scraps of wood/MDF (24 off);
- MDF-compatible screws (8 off).

First, lay newspaper on your work surface to protect from glue drips and so on.

Lay one mould section onto the paper and insert four 8mm dowels into just one of each of the paired holes. Apply glue to the surface of the mould section and to the dowels, position another section over the first, ensuring the dowels locate properly, and tap down onto the first section. Insert four further 8mm dowels into the unused holes, apply a thin layer of glue to the surface of the second mould section and to the dowels and position a further section over the second, ensuring the dowels locate properly, and tap down. Insert four dowels into the same hole used by the original dowels, and glue and tap down a fourth section.

Clamp across all four sections with the G-clamps, sliding scrap pieces of wood between the clamps and the mould to increase the clamping area and also to avoid damaging the mould's surface. Ensure that you clamp with even pressure, that all four sections are gap-free and that a small bead of glue squeeze-out is evident.

Repeat the above procedure with the remaining four mould sections to make the other half of the mould. Allow to dry thoroughly, unclamp and clean up all glue squeeze-out with a sharp scraper.

You should now have two identical halves of a mould. Make sure that both halves butt up together precisely; clean up and square up the mating faces if required. These can be joined together with a square of wood, drilled through and secured with four MDF-compatible screws.

The mould, including the removable cutaway block.

The mould pieces being glued together.

If the guitar is going to have a cutaway, the block can be fashioned from an offcut of the MDF blocks and screwed to the mould. In this way, it can be removed to allow a non-cutaway instrument to be constructed using the same mould.

The Soundboard and Back Arch Templates

The Bracing Arch Templates

Neither the soundboard nor the back of the guitars featured here are flat, but are formed into a gentle dome. To maintain that arched profile the bottom edge of each major brace (the surface to be glued) has a curve planed into it. For the guitars in this book, the soundboard has a 3mm (⅛in) arch, and the back has a 6mm (¼in) arch.

The Soundboard Arch (1.5mm) Template

This is used for the transverse brace and the tone bars.

Materials required
- Aeroply: 560mm (22in) *(L)* × 50mm (2in) *(W)* × 0.8mm *(T)*;
- a handle/stiffener: 560mm (22in);
- a 600mm (24in) rule;
- panel pins.

Draw a line on the aeroply parallel to one long edge and 3mm (⅛in) in from that edge. Draw a second line parallel to the first so that the lines are 1.5mm (¹⁄₁₆in) apart. Drill two holes that are just big enough for the diameter of the pins being used along this second line, placing them 535mm (21in) apart and 12.7mm (½in) in from each end. Drill the holes with the edges touching but not centred on the line.

Lay the aeroply on a piece of scrap wood and hammer a pin into each hole. Mount the 600mm (24in) rule so that it spans the two pins and push the centre of the rule so that it touches the first line. Hold securely, and draw the curve formed by the rule onto the ply.

This line represents a 1.5mm (¹⁄₁₆in) deflection over 535mm (21in). Cut close to the line and then trim accurately to it with a sharp knife, a file or a block plane on a **shooting** board.

Glue the handle onto the other long edge to provide stiffness and ease of use. Mark onto the template with indelible pen the centre of the arch and the label '1.5mm Brace Arch Template'.

The Soundboard Arch (3mm) Template

This is used for the X-brace.

Materials required:
- Aeroply: 560mm (22in) *(L)* × 50mm (2in) *(W)* × 0.8mm *(T)*;
- a handle/stiffener: 560mm (22in);
- a 600mm (24in) rule;
- panel pins.

Draw a line on the aeroply parallel to one long edge and 3mm (⅛in) from that edge. Draw a second line parallel to the first so that the lines are 3mm (⅛in) apart. Drill two holes that are just big enough for the diameter of the pins being used along this second line, placing them 535mm (21in) apart and 12.7mm (½in) in from each end. Drill the holes with the edges touching but not centred on the line.

Lay the aeroply on a piece of scrap wood and hammer a pin into each hole. Mount the 600mm (24in) rule so that it spans the two pins and push the centre of the rule so that it touches the first line. Hold securely, and draw the curve formed by the rule onto the ply.

This line represents a 3mm (⅛in) deflection over 535mm (21in). Cut close to the line and then trim accurately to it with a sharp knife, a file or a block plane on a shooting board.

Glue the handle onto the other long edge to provide stiffness and ease of use. Mark onto the template with indelible pen the centre of the arch and the label '3mm Brace Arch Template'.

The Back Arch (6mm) Template

This is used for all four of the back braces.

Materials required
- Aeroply: 560mm (22in) *(L)* × 50mm (2in) *(W)* × 0.8mm *(T)*;
- a handle/stiffener: 560mm (22in);
- a 600mm (24in) rule;
- panel pins.

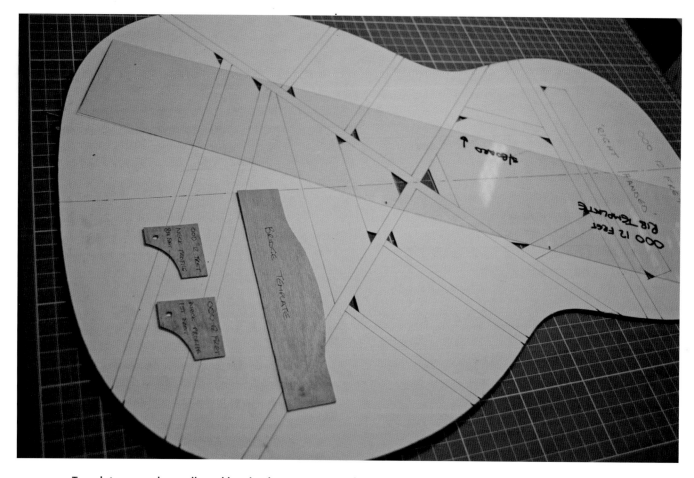

Templates: a card soundboard bracing layout, acetate rib arch profile, and bridge and neck shape templates.

Draw a line on the aeroply parallel to one long edge and 3mm (⅛in) in from that edge. Draw a second line parallel to the first so that the lines are 6mm (¼in) apart. Drill two holes that are just big enough for the diameter of the pins being used along this second line, placing them 535mm (21in) apart and 12.7mm (½in) in from each end. Drill the holes with the edges touching but not centred on the line.

Lay the aeroply on a piece of scrap wood and hammer a pin into each hole. Mount the 600mm (24in) rule so that it spans the two pin, and push the centre of the rule so that it touches the first line. Hold securely, and draw the curve formed by the rule onto the ply.

This line represents a 6mm (¼in) deflection over 535mm (21in). Cut close to the line and then trim accurately to it with a sharp knife, a file or a block plane on a shooting board.

Glue the handle onto the other long edge for stiffness and ease of use. Mark onto the template with indelible

pen the centre of the arch and the label '6mm Brace Arch Template'.

Other templates are also recommended and will be mentioned throughout the book.

Woods Used for the Guitars in this Book

Cutting List for the 000 Twelve-Fret Guitar

The following list is relevant to the making of the 000 **twelve-fret** guitar as illustrated in this book, so the measurements relate to this model of guitar. If you are making an alternative model then the measurements need to be amended to suit.

Component	Quantity	Minimum Measurements (L) × (W) × (T)
Soundboard	2	546mm (21½in) × 203mm (8in) × 5mm (³⁄₁₆in)
Back	2	546mm (21½in) × 203mm (8in) × 5mm (³⁄₁₆in)
Ribs	2	840mm (33in) × 105mm (4³⁄₁₆in) × 3mm (⅛in)
Neck	1	800mm (31½in) × 75mm (3in) × 25mm (1in)
Headstock veneer	1	170mm (6¾in) × 75mm (3in) × 3mm (⅛in)
Fingerboard	1	460mm (18in) × 63.5mm (2½in) × 6mm (¼in)
Bridge blank	1	160mm (6¼in) × 30mm (1³⁄₁₆in) × 12.7mm (½in)
Neck block	1	85mm (3⅜in) × 75mm (3in) × 35mm (1³⁄₈in)
Tail block	1	105mm (4³⁄₁₆in) × 80mm (3⅛in) × 20mm (²⁵⁄₃₂in)
Soundboard and back bracing		See separate lists in later sections 'The Soundboard Braces and Tone Bars' and 'The Back'.

The Basic Neck Construction

Notes on the Headstock Angle

See Chapter 7 for a full explanation of the correct string path/angle over the **nut** and so on, but a brief explanation is useful here for determining the ideal headstock angle.

THE SOLID HEADSTOCK

This type is by far the most common on steel string guitars and is where the **machinehead**s are mounted from the rear of the headstock and generally only require six holes drilled through the wood to accommodate them. Once a string passes over the nut via its individual slot it needs to travel in a downward path to its machinehead roller. This ensures that the string is held down securely and has positive contact with the slot. The angle at which the string leaves the nut will determine how effective this is – if the angle is too shallow the string will have a tendency to bounce in the slot, if too acute the added friction will cause **intonation** and tuning problems. An angle of 14–15 degrees is commonly agreed to be ideal for a solid headstock.

THE SLOTTED HEADSTOCK

This type is more common on classical nylon string guitars, but it is used on smaller parlour and 00/000 type steel string guitars. The machineheads are mounted from the sides of the headstock and the strings gain access to their rollers through an elongated slot (each one usually accessing three machineheads). The string contact point on these rollers is lower in relation to the headstock face than for a rear-mounted type, so if a headstock pitch of 15 degrees is maintained the string will leave the nut at a more acute angle. Therefore, the headstock angle can be made shallower to compensate, commonly at 10 degrees. *(Remember to take into account that the shallower the angle, the longer the scarf joint will be.)*

Materials required

- Timber: 900mm (35⁷⁄₁₆in) *(L)* × 75mm (3in) *(W)* × 25mm (1in) *(T)*

Neck blank components showing the headstock and heel pieces.

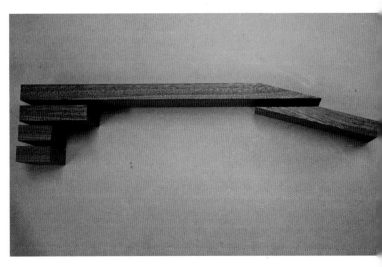

A headstock scarf joint angle being cut on a purpose-built jig on a bandsaw.

The neck blank and headstock blank mounted in a planing jig.

Plane the timber so that you have a blank that is flat, smooth, square and parallel (*see* 'Preparing a Timber Blank' in Chapter 1).

Mark in 180mm from one end of Face A and draw a pencil line across the face at 90 degrees to Face B. From this line set a protractor to the relevant headstock angle and draw a another line at this angle across Face B and Face C.

Set up the fence on the bandsaw such that the slot of the headstock cutting jig is central to the saw blade. Mount the neck blank onto the jig, ensuring that the angle line is also centred on the blade. Secure the blank with a G-clamp, padded out with a wooden caul to avoid indentation.

Slowly run the jig along the fence to feed the blank into the saw blade, cutting the headstock angle precisely. The two freshly cut faces now need to be planed perfectly smooth, flat and square, so mount both pieces onto the headstock planing jig as described.

It is important that the vulnerable edge of the main neck blank is resting precisely at the edge of the jig, such that it is fully supported but the jig doesn't impede the path of the plane. Also ensure that the equally vulnerable edge of the headstock blank is lined up with the neck blank angle. Secure all together with the threaded clamp, which should be sited back far enough to avoid contact with the back of the plane.

With a very sharp plane smooth down both faces, taking very fine shavings. Check regularly with a straight edge and an engineer's square that these faces are flat and that they remain at 90 degrees to the neck blank. Set a sliding bevel to the required angle of the headstock and check that the cut faces remain at that angle.

The headstock section now requires planing to the required thickness. This should be the total depth minus the thickness of the face veneer. Score a line with a marking gauge to denote this measurement and plane down to it.

Hold the headstock section in position under the neck blank and determine that it is a precise fit. If there are any gaps, or you can rock the section from side to side, it is not ready to fit. Check and correct the surfaces if they need further flattening (*see* 'Luthiery Essentials' in the Introduction). If you can rock the joint from side to side, check not only the surface of the headstock scarf for flatness but also the underside of the neck blank.

Mount the neck blank on the headstock gluing jig on edge and position the headstock section in place, ensuring that the neck blank angle and headstock are aligned and that the headstock section is butted up against the jig's block. Secure the neck blank to the jig with two wooden cam clamps. Assemble wooden cauls with non-stick paper either side of

The rough-sawn faces of the neck and headstock blank being planed flat and smooth.

The fully planed headstock and neck blank scarf joint angle.

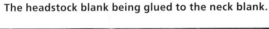

The headstock blank being glued to the neck blank.

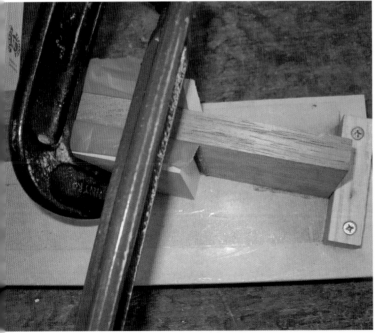

the joint and hold all together with two G-clamps. Check one last time that the joint is aligned and gap-free, remove the clamps and then apply sufficient glue to the headstock section angle, reassemble and re-clamp. Ensure that the parts are still aligned and have not slid out of position. Leave to cure thoroughly.

GOOD PRACTICE ADVICE: GLUING THE HEADSTOCK AND NECK BLANK

- The clamps are essentially holding the two sections together whilst the glue dries, and should not be employed to force an ill-fitting joint together (see 'Good Techniques' section in Chapter 1).
- A sign of a good-fitting joint is a thin bead of glue squeeze-out.
- To help avoid any excessive slippage, once glue is applied rub the headstock piece back and forth on the neck blank until you feel the glue begin to grab.

Heel Assembly

Materials required

- Neck offcut measuring 100mm (4in) (L) × 75mm (3in) (W) × 25mm (1in) (T) (1 off);
- neck offcuts measuring 63.5mm (2½in) (L) × 75mm (3in) (W) × 25mm (1in) (T) (2 off).

The neck heel is made up of three pieces, cut from the original neck blank. Cut the heel pieces in sequence and orientate them in the same direction. Again, ensure that all mating surfaces are an exact fit (*see* 'Good Techniques' section in Chapter 1) and number each piece to assist with assembly and gluing.

With the neck blank still mounted on the gluing jig, assemble the heel pieces, place wooden cauls either side of the assembly, and hold together with three G-clamps. Check one last time that the joints are aligned and gap-free, remove the clamps, apply glue to one surface of each heel piece, then reassemble and re-clamp.

GLUING THE NECK HEEL

When glue has been applied, there is a tendency for each piece to want to slide apart from the others. This can be reduced by employing the technique of a 'rub joint'. As you assemble each piece, rub the two mating surfaces together until you feel the glue begin to grab. Make sure that the section is in its ideal position when this happens.

Ensure all parts are aligned and have not slid out of position. It may also be necessary to clamp over the top of the whole assembly to prevent the heel pieces from rising up. Leave to cure thoroughly.

Routing the Truss Rod Slot

Equipment required

- A router combined with adjustable fence;
- a router cutter (with same diameter as the width of the truss rod).

Ensure that the neck blank assembly has parallel sides, and that the headstock section and heel assembly are flush with

The heel pieces being glued together on a purpose-built jig.

the neck section. Mark one side that is proven flat and square to the neck's surface as the datum edge.

Set a marking gauge to half the neck blank's width and scribe a line down its face from the datum edge. This will now denote the neck's centre line.

Mount the neck assembly securely, with the heel in a vice and the headstock clamped to the bench. Set up the router so that with its fence placed against the datum edge the centre of the router cutter is aligned with the centre line of the neck. Set the router's depth stop so that you cannot rout deeper than prescribed.

Before routing the slot, make sure that the router is supported fully along the length of the neck blank. If it is unstable at either end due to having insufficient surface to rest on, clamp a scrap piece of wood to the bench at the same level as the neck to keep the router steady.

Rout a slot to the required depth, ensuring that the fence is in constant touch with the datum edge. Plunge the router cutter only 2–3mm (⅛in) at a time, to avoid over-straining the router and to help obtain a constant and straight slot. Double-check the depth of the slot by measuring with a vernier gauge.

The Headstock Veneer

The **headstock veneer** serves more than one function. Not only does it enliven what can be a bland-looking headstock face by utilizing a contrasting wood, it also covers and strengthens the visible scarf joint line and forms the back edge of the nut slot.

First, check that the neck blank angle and the headstock

The headstock veneer pinned in place against a dummy nut.

face are perfectly flat. If there is any discrepancy, level with a sharp block plane. Try not to obliterate the headstock angle line (the rear-of-nut position), which should remain a crisp and square junction.

Draw a centre line down the face and also across the top edge of the headstock. Clamp a piece of square-edged wood precisely at the headstock angle (this will represent a dummy nut).

One narrow edge of the headstock veneer needs to be planed at an appropriate angle, such that when offered up to the dummy nut it fits precisely and gap-free. This can be achieved by laying the veneer on the bench hook/small shooting board and by tipping a block plane on edge, creating a bevel on the edge of the veneer. Keep offering this up against the dummy nut until the angle is correct with the veneer lying flat on the face of the headstock.

To ensure that the veneer does not slip out of position whilst gluing, it needs to be held in place by a couple of panel pins. Drill two holes in the veneer opposite each other, of a diameter to be a snug fit for the pins. Drill these holes either in the waste area outside the finished headstock profile or where the machinehead holes or slots will eventually be created.

The headstock veneer being glued in place: note the wooden cauls at the top and bottom of headstock.

The headstock veneers glued on for both neck blanks.

It is advisable to affix tape to the headstock to allow accurate cutting on dark woods.

Shaping the Headstock

Re-instate a centre line down the centre of the headstock face by joining the line on the neck blank and the line on the top edge of the headstock. Position the relevant template on this centre line and draw on accurately the headstock profile, the centres of all the machinehead holes and so on.

The profile needs to be cut out precisely, ensuring that the edges are square to the headstock face. To be able to see the lines marked onto dark wood veneers it is advisable to stick masking tape temporarily along these lines whilst passing it through the bandsaw.

Plane and file the edges of the headstock smooth, 90 degrees to the veneer face and accurately to the line.

SOLID HEADSTOCKS

Centre-punch the machinehead hole positions and drill them out carefully. It is advisable to drill a pilot hole initially and then bore a hole with the appropriate size bit from the front most of the way through, and then from the back. This avoids drill breakout and damage to the edges of the holes. Counterbore these holes if the machineheads you are using come complete with mounting bushes.

Position the veneer and push the pins through the holes to indent the surface of the headstock.

Remove the veneer, and drill the indentations 3mm (⅛in) deep with a drill bit of the same diameter. Apply sufficient glue to the surface of the headstock, reapply the veneer and lock it in place by pushing the pins through the veneer and into the shallow holes in the headstock. Lay a wooden caul over the veneer (having previously drilled clearance holes in this to pass over the panel pins) and another caul behind the headstock, and clamp all together with four to six G-clamps.

Having allowed the glue to dry thoroughly, trim back any excess veneer flush to the sides of the headstock.

Headstocks taking shape.

Machinehead roller holes being drilled on the drill press.

SLOTTED HEADSTOCKS

The machinehead roller holes need first to be drilled accurately. Mark the position of the first roller on either side of the headstock. Mark from this to the middle roller, and then from the first to the third roller position and then centre-punch. Mount the headstock in a drill vice, such that the edge is at 90 degrees to the appropriately sized drill bit.

Measure the length of the machinehead roller and put a tape marker on the bit to prevent drilling too deep. Carefully drill the three holes and try the machineheads to determine that the holes are deep enough. Turn the headstock over to the other edge and set it up so that it is at 90 degrees to the drill bit. Drill the other three holes and check that they too are deep enough.

Machinehead slot drilling jig showing the backstop and drilling board.

DRILLING MACHINEHEAD ROLLER HOLES

It is not unusual when drilling the machinehead roller holes from each side of a slotted headstock that they break into each other, especially the two lowest ones. If you are at all unsure about this operation, it is worthwhile making a three-hole jig out of a piece of hardwood to drill the roller holes accurately.

Machinehead slots being drilled out with a Forstner bit on the drill press.

Machineheads slots being scored with a knife to achieve a straight edge.

Machinehead slots drilled and scored, awaiting chiselling.

Machinehead slots being cleaned up from the front with a chisel.

Machinehead slots being cleaned up from the back with a chisel.

The machinehead string roller slots now need to be fashioned. If they are going to be drilled out then it is advised that a Forstner bit is used. These types drill a very clean hole and, if used carefully, will not cause significant break-out when passed through the headstock.

Set up a flat piece of hardwood on the drill press and clamp onto the drill table a straight backstop along which the headstock edge will run. In this way, all of the holes will be in line with each other.

Mark the centres of the first and last holes (the extremes of the slot) and drill through from the back, ensuring that the veneered face of the headstock is held firmly down on the hardwood piece. Bore further holes, overlapping each one so that you end up with a largely excavated slot. Next, score a line joining all of the edges of the holes to outline the slot.

Carefully pare down with a wide sharp chisel, removing the excess wood, halfway into the slot and until the edges are straight and clean. Turn the headstock over, join the edges of the holes with a scored line in the same way as for the other side and pare down with a chisel, meeting the cut face from the front.

These operations are also possible by using a specialist jig and a router.

Machinehead roller holes being drilled on a purpose-bought jig.

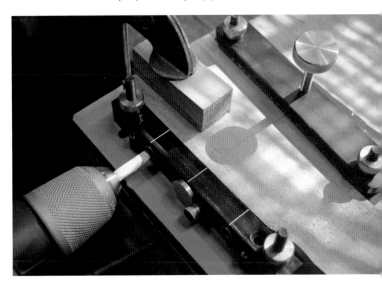

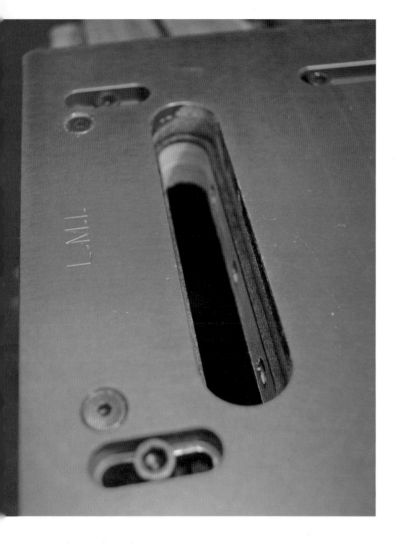

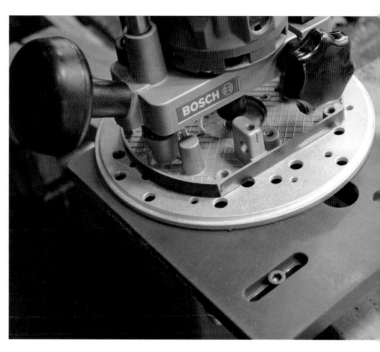

A machinehead slot routing jig and router.

A machinehead slot being routed using a purpose-bought jig.

Filing the string slot, angled down towards the headstock.

Three neck blanks – the bottom one retains its centre portion for ease of clamping.

The path the first and sixth strings take from the back of the nut to their respective machinehead rollers is commonly at such an angle that they would snag on the wood at the edge of the slot if it was left flat. Therefore, it is usual to ramp down the leading edge of these slots with a round file.

Shaping the Back of the Neck

THE NECK PROFILE

Before the neck is attached to the body it is advisable to at least shape the heel, the transition from the heel to the back of the neck, the neck profile at the first fret position and also its transition to the back of the headstock. These are jobs that are easier to complete whilst the neck is a separate assembly. The remainder of the neck can be left flat and square, which enables it to be held securely in a vice, which also serves as a solid base for the fretting process.

The necks on the guitars shown here were fully shaped whilst they were separate units. The reason for this is because when you remove a relatively substantial amount of wood from a length of timber, it can cause the wood to move slightly. This could result in the top surface of the neck no longer being dead flat. If this occurs then it can be rectified easily by lightly planing it level again. Having a fully profiled back to the neck does mean that specially shaped blocks have

to be made to support the neck whilst fretting, but once made these can be used many times over.

There are various shapes or profiles to which the back of the neck can be carved (commonly known as V-shape, C-shape, D-shape, and so on); these are often dependant on personal taste and playing style. If there is a neck shape you wish to copy, it is possible to reproduce it utilizing a profile gauge and transposing this to a piece of template material. Generally neck profiles are symmetrical, so they only require a half template (that is, from the centre line of the neck to the edge of the fingerboard). Two templates are required: one for the neck profile at the first fret position and one for the eighth fret position (for twelve-fret necks) or the tenth fret position (for fourteen-fret necks).

Reinstate a pencilled centre line down the back of the neck and heel. This needs to remain visible and undisturbed throughout the carving process, to ensure that the maximum thickness of the neck is retained. On the top surface of the neck, accurately mark on the neck taper from the nut to the neck/body joint. Ensure that the taper is equidistant either side of the centre line.

Mark the point at which the neck joins the body (usually at the twelfth or fourteenth fret position).

Remember to allow for the thickness of the nut in the calculation. Mark across this point with an engineer's square from the datum edge and down both sides of the heel. If an add-on

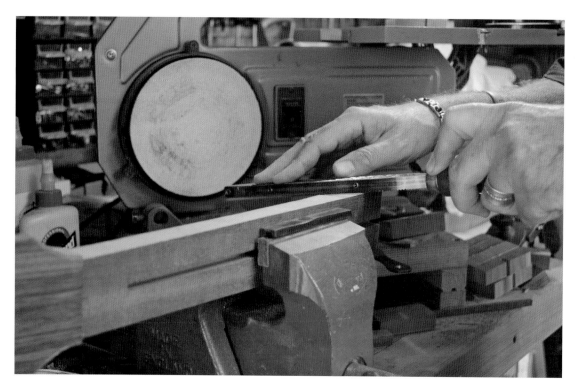

Rough-shaping the heel profile with a Japanese saw file.

tenon is going to be employed (as detailed here), cut off any excess just shy of this line. If an integral dovetail or tenon has been decided on then sufficient length needs to be added to allow for this.

Using the side profile template, draw on the side outline, giving special attention to the curve from the back of the neck to the heel. (This is where the template comes into its own and proves its worth by avoiding any major miscalculations and incorrect cutting). Cut away the waste area to within 1mm of the line. If the heel curve is too tight for the bandsaw you are using, cut parallel cuts up to the curved profile, and then cut away the waste. This will leave a ridged finish, but it will be easy enough to smooth down with files.

Cut the neck taper waste from the heel end to the headstock transition. Place a scrap block of wood the same height as the heel stack under the headstock end of the neck blank when passing it through the bandsaw to support the neck safely.

If the heel sides are to be tapered, mark this profile on the back face of the heel and cut away any excess almost to the heel taper line. Smooth down to the line with either a plane or a file such as a Japanese saw rasp.

Clamp the neck so that it protrudes from the bench for easy access. An excavation approximately 25mm (1in) wide should

The neck profile being roughed-out at the neck/headstock transition.

The two neck profile points can now be joined up by carving the intervening section with a spokeshave. Bear in mind that the neck will taper in thickness from the headstock to the heel, so check regularly that you are not cutting below the required surface. One way to help with this process is to cut away from you with the spokeshave for a few passes, then turn the spokeshave around and cut towards you. There is a tendency that cutting away results in a hollowing of the work but when pulling towards you the tendency is to arch the cut. By regularly reversing the procedure, the hollowing and arching tend to even out.

Bear in mind when checking for flatness that the neck shape is a cone, so it will not read flat if measured parallel to the centre line.

The neck profile being roughed-out at the neck/heel transition.

be cut behind the first fret area to define the neck profile at this point. Using gouges or rasps, cut up from one side of the neck in a circular fashion towards the centre line.

Keep checking with the half template that the shape being carved is consistent with the template shape. When you are happy that this is so, carve up from the opposite side towards the centre line, again regularly checking with the template, until this side is identical to the first. Repeat this procedure at the eighth fret position (for twelve-fret necks) or the tenth fret position (for fourteen-fret necks).

The neck profile is now clearly defined at two points (adjacent to the headstock and also to the heel).

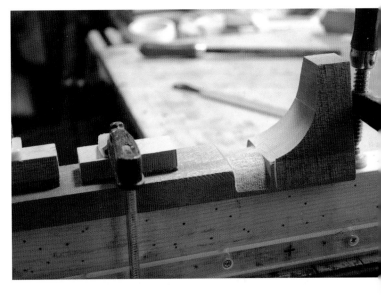

The neck/heel transition profile cut in.

The neck/headstock transition profile cut in.

Checking the neck profile against the template.

The neck profiles being joined up with a spokeshave: cutting away.

The neck profiles being joined up with a spokeshave: cutting towards.

One half of the neck profiled.

Both halves of neck profiled – note the purpose-made straight edge.

The bottom of the heel profile marked out.

Carving the heel/neck stem transition.

THE HEEL PROFILE

The heel on Guitar #1 has parallel sides, with one side sitting flush with the cutaway. This serves to cover the end of the cutaway rib where it butts up against the main rib. It is possible to carve a tapered heel in this situation, but it is argued that the square heel makes for a more comfortable hand position when in the cutaway area (it is not pressed against the sharp edge where the two ribs meet).

The heel on Guitar #2 has tapered sides, which is a more traditional profile. If this shape is decided on, be aware that the taper should not be so extreme as to expose any of the mortice slot.

It is also traditional for the bottom of the heel to be finished off with a **heel cap**, often in the same wood as the binding. This can be affixed after the neck is assembled to the body. If the heel is to be tapered, mount the neck blank in a padded vice and clamp the neck so that it protrudes from the bench for easy access to the heel.

Working from either side of the heel, carve towards the centre of the heel's front face. This can be done with rasps or gouges, to rough out the initial shape. When close to the desired profile, revert to carving knives, files and scrapers to smooth out the surface. This then needs to be blended in to the neck profile already carved, just forward of the heel.

The heel carve: note the layers of tape on the neck stem to protect from accidental knife slip.

Carving the headstock/neck stem transition.

An obvious lump between the neck arm profile and the heel, which should be a more gently curved transition.

CARVING THE HEADSTOCK/NECK TRANSITION

The flat back of the headstock needs to be blended into the neck profile already carved behind the first fret position. A good place to begin the carving is where the headstock flares out from the nut position to a point. Carefully cut a facet from this point down to the neck profile, removing just enough excess wood to blend it into the neck profile. Use a carving knife or round files to achieve this.

To ensure that the neck carve is consistent and lump-free, hold the neck up horizontally and slowly rotate it whilst looking from one end to the other. This is a good visual check, as any substantial dips or lumps should become fairly obvious. Mark them with a pencil and refine them until they blend in with the rest of the neck.

It is also worthwhile smoothing all of the surfaces whilst the neck is detached from the body. To help create a very regular and even back to the neck, it is recommended that a strip of abrasive is cut, held at each end and pulled over the neck contour. Pulling it up and down 'shoe shine' fashion should even out any facets or ridges. Do not overwork any one area, as this will create a dip or hollow, but lightly sand whilst moving the abrasive up and down the neck.

The neck assembly can now be put to one side whilst you work on the other components.

The Soundboard

Soundboard Joining

Soundboards are supplied in two book-matched halves and are usually 5–6mm (¼in) thick. These two halves require gluing together, which is best done whilst they are this thick. The reason for this is that if the surfaces of each half become slightly misaligned during the gluing process, it is still possible to level them and have sufficient final thickness.

Lay out the two halves with the long edges butted together to identify their correct orientation. The suppliers often mark each half to help with this but, if in any doubt, each half should mirror the other. Notice also that the growth lines are generally closer together at the side of the half board and get increasingly wider apart towards the other edge. The side to be joined should be the one adjacent to the growth lines that are closest together. Mark across both halves with a cross as a reminder of the correct orientation.

As the join is going to be a butt join (not mechanically linked but relying solely on the glue), the two edges need to be smoothed and straightened very accurately to form

Cumpiano this explains so much better — All too vague!! [handwritten annotation]

a perfect gap-free join. This is achieved by the following method.

SHOOTING THE EDGES
Equipment required
- The shooting board;
- a long wooden plane;
- a good light source.

Very lightly plane smooth the surface of each soundboard half adjacent to the edge to be joined. This will help with determining a good fit and will stop any errant raised wood fibres becoming trapped in the join. Close the two halves together as if closing a book and lay them onto the shooting board, with the edge to be planed overhanging the edge of the top portion by 5–6mm (¼in).

KEEPING THE SOUNDBOARD HALVES TOGETHER

It is important to maintain the soundboard halves in this orientation. If the plane blade or the plane body itself is not exactly square, it will put a very slight angle on the two faces. However, when opened out and butted together, any discrepancy will be cancelled out.

NB Secure!! Wood would move!! [handwritten annotation]

Lay the plane on its side and use the long sole of the plane to align both edges. With one hand hold the soundboard halves firmly in position and with the other hand hold the plane in its centre over the blade. Smoothly but firmly plane (**shoot**) the edges from one end to the other.

Repeat until you are getting a fine shaving along the whole length of both pieces. It is now important to check for a good fit, which can be done in a couple of ways: *Setting of plane not described.* [handwritten annotation]

The light test Hold both halves firmly together against a good light source (on a good bright day, flat onto the glass of a window, or, if you have one, a light box) and determine if there is any light visible along the whole length of the join.

The friction test Butt both halves together on a flat surface with the outer edge nearest you against a support (your stomach will do) and hold both halves firmly together. Slightly lift one end of one half and observe the other half. If it too lifts, then it is touching and is a good fit. If the second half stays put, there is a gap and more planing is required.

Push along the join on one half and again observe the other. If it is a good fit, both halves will move together. If one half moves, but the second half remains stationary, there is a gap.

It will soon become apparent that only a very small imperfection can make the difference between a good fit and an

Shooting the edges of the soundboard halves.

Checking soundboard edges for gaps by lifting up one half.

Checking the soundboard edges for gaps by pressing on one half.

[handwritten: bit late now saying this!]

unacceptable gap, so for this reason it is necessary to back off the plane blade so that only extremely fine shavings are evident. Mark the places that are a good fit, and plane very fine shavings off these areas. This way the sections containing gaps should eventually begin to fit.

[handwritten: misunderstand idea of shooting board!!!]

ERADICATE ALL GAPS

Any gaps that have been identified will, if left that way, translate into ugly glue lines and also weak spots in the join.

Once you can be assured that the *whole length* of the join is fitting perfectly, it needs to be glued. This should be done directly following the planing, as if left for a period of time any small movements of the timber in the interim would render the join unsatisfactory and require further correction.

PLANING ADVICE

If you have experienced any difficulty planing both halves together, they can be planed individually but remember to keep them in the correct orientation (that is, one half facing up, the other facing down).

The Soundboard/Back Join Gluing Board

Lay out both soundboard halves onto the board, with the outer edge of one half overhanging the square holes along the board's edge. Adjust the back stop to butt up against the outer edge of the other half. Hold the centre join to prevent it rising up and insert the wedges firmly into the square holes. Check the join one last time for a good fit.

If satisfied that this is so, remove the wedges and fold the halves together. Apply a bead of glue down both edges to be joined and smooth it out with a clean finger. Re-lay the halves onto the board, holding the centre join whilst re-inserting wedges, and ensure the surfaces of both halves are as level with each other as possible. Still holding down the soundboard halves, lay a folded sheet of newspaper over the join and place weights on top of it to prevent the join from rising up.

Gluing the back halves together on a purpose-built jig.

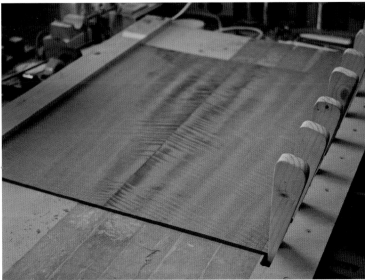

[handwritten: Must have spent 1/2 his life making jigs (or got the students to do it)]

63

Sash Clamp Joining

An alternative method of gluing the soundboard halves together is by employing three sash clamps. Lay the clamps onto the bench, with the outer ones spread a suitable distance apart to accommodate the length of the soundboard and the third one in the centre. Lay a sheet of folded newspaper across the centre of the clamps, lay both halves of the soundboard onto the clamps and tighten sufficiently to hold them together. Hold down the join whilst doing this to avoid it rising up. Check the join one last time to ascertain that it is a good fit.

If satisfied that this is so, release the clamps and fold the two halves together. Apply a bead of glue down both edges to be joined and smooth it out with a clean finger. Re-lay the soundboard halves onto the clamps and hold the centre join whilst tightening them, ensuring the surfaces of both halves are as level with each other as possible. Still holding down the soundboard halves, lay a folded sheet of newspaper over the join and place weights on top of it to prevent the join rising up.

CLAMPING PRESSURE

When using either the wedge method or the sash clamp method, the clamping pressure should be adequate to hold both soundboard halves together whilst the glue cures but not to force an ill-fitting join together.

Levelling and Thicknessing the Joined Soundboard

Even though the soundboard halves were joined whilst at their thickest, the chances are that the surfaces of both halves are not perfectly level with each other. This means that sufficient wood has to be planed off to achieve a flat surface. With an initial target figure of 3mm (⅛in) thickness, this does not allow for the removal of vast amounts of timber.

With this in mind, once again use plane blades that are as sharp as possible, to enable very fine shavings. This is also important as, although the soundboard is a softwood, the sharpest possible blade will prevent tear-out and will give you a surface that will need no further smoothing.

The joined soundboard needs to be clamped securely to a flat surface. Any glue squeeze-out and remnants of newspaper should first be removed. Planing dried glue is detrimental to plane blades, so using a sharp scraper is preferable. The whole surface should then be lightly planed level. First determine in which direction the soundboard wood planes best. It is not unusual to get grain tear-out in one direction; if this happens, plane from the opposite direction by turning the soundboard around. It is also common to discover that each half requires planing from a different direction. This is due to a certain amount of grain runout as a consequence of the way the timber was initially cut or how it has grown. With this in mind, it is a good idea to plane first across the grain to level the width, then plane diagonally and then with the grain to smooth completely.

Planing the soundboard surface flat and smooth.

GOOD PRACTICE ADVICE: PLANING THE SOUNDBOARD

- It is good practice to re-sharpen the blade for the last operation to ensure the finest of shavings to give a perfectly smooth finish.
- Remember to always round off the corners of the plane's blade to prevent it digging in to the wood's surface.
- Ensure that the board on which the soundboard is placed is swept clean regularly. As the soundboard is a soft wood, it is very easy to dent it with carelessly discarded shavings, chippings, old glue and so on.
- If you discover inadvertent dents to the wood's surface, drop a small amount of warm water onto it. This should swell the wood fibres enough to level them with the face.
- Depending upon the finish you intend to apply, you may wish to save some shavings from the soundboard for burnishing the finished product (*see* 'A Method for Finishing Early Guitars' in Chapter 6).

When you are satisfied that you have prepared the first surface as perfectly as you possibly can, turn the soundboard over and repeat the above process on the other side.

When both sides are planed, determine which side will be your show face. This is quite often decided by one side of the join looking better than the other, or having a wood grain that is more consistent. If there are going to be any issues with the quality of the soundboard's surface, ensure that they will be on the inside (although having said that, ideally the inside face should be as good as the outside).

CARE WITH EACH COMPONENT

Try not to fall into the habit of thinking that the areas of any components that are not readily seen should not have the same care and consideration as those that are. Apart from being bad practice, a less than ideal surface can be detrimental to a good gluing surface and can even affect the performance.

Measure the soundboard's thickness all over. As previously stated, the aim is an initial target figure of 3mm (⅛in). If the soundboard is thicker than this it can be reduced by planing more off the inside face. It has already been discussed that the ideal soundboard thickness for any piece of timber is more to do with its stiffness and other properties than one universal measurement.

This is a good point at which to try and determine the stiffness of the soundboard. Hold it along its lower edge and flex it across its width. It should bend but still feel like it is relatively resistant. What you do not want is for the soundboard to feel like a piece of card – flaccid and floppy.

Next hold the uppermost edge lightly between thumb and forefinger, hold it up to one ear and tap across its surface with the knuckle of your middle finger on your other hand. What you ideally want to hear is a ring to the knock, with a certain amount of sustain. If you get a dull thud, the chances are that the soundboard is too thick and needs thinning out more.

TESTING SOUNDBOARD THICKNESS

Determining ideal thickness using the above methods takes time to master, but the earlier you start and the more you practise it the quicker you will gain an understanding of the process.

Before you achieve the final thickness of the soundboard, and whilst it is still at approximately 3mm (⅛in) thick, it is a good idea to install the soundhole surround inlay.

The Soundhole Inlay

The inlay surrounding the soundhole is not only decorative but serves a purpose by helping to reinforce the border of a relatively large hole.

What goes into the inlay is largely a matter of taste. Look at as many examples as possible on other instruments to get an idea of proportion and complexity before deciding what type of design to use. It can in fact be detrimental to the performance of the soundboard if the inlay encroaches too far into the resonant area of the top, so work on the principal of 'less is more' – keeping it simple is often the best outcome.

The traditional surround on 'classical' guitars is a very intricate construction of tiny mosaic squares, which can be very ornate but is extremely time consuming to make. If you decide that this is the type you wish to imitate, then there are very good details of how these can be achieved in Roy Courtnall's *Making Master Guitars* (Hale, 1993), William R. Cumpiano

Baroque guitar (built by the author) soundhole inlay and carved rose.

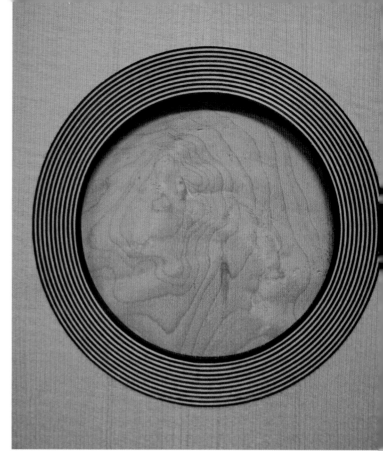

The soundhole surround from a nineteenth-century style guitar after R. Lacote (built by the author).

The soundhole surround from a nineteenth-century style guitar after L. Panormo (built by the author).

and Jonathan D. Natelson's *Guitar Making* (Chronicle Books, 1994) and other titles (*see* Suggested Further Reading).

The following describes two methods of inlay more traditionally employed on steel string guitars. Whatever you decide, making your own is far more satisfying than purchasing a shop-bought item.

MAKING YOUR OWN VENEER LINES

Although veneer thickness lines can be purchased ready-made, you can easily make your own from off-cuts of the timber you are utilizing in the making process. This way you can guarantee a good colour match with the other components on your guitar and you have much more control over the size and thickness of these lines.

Ideally you need to cut the strips for the lines from quarter-sawn wood rather than slab-sawn (this is especially true for open grain woods like mahogany, and even maple). As the soundhole surround is inlaid into the soundboard by approximately half its thickness, the lines need to be wide enough to give enough depth to the surround such that it will sit proud of the routed slot to allow for any irregularities.

Rough cut the inlay line blanks to 3mm (⅛in) *(W)* × 1.5mm (¹⁄₁₆in) *(T)*. Their length should be adequate to encircle the maximum circumference of the surround, plus a bit extra to allow for breakages and corrections.

PLANING ADVICE

*If you plane the edge of the off-cut each time you saw a rough-cut line, each line will already have one face that is smooth and flat so only one face will require running through the **thicknesser**.*

THICKNESSING THE VENEER LINES

The blade in the thicknesser is used more as a scraper than a cutter and it should be sharpened regularly to provide a good keen edge.

To set up the thicknesser place a veneer line, rough-sawn face uppermost, on to the base and lower the cutter to just touch the surface of the line. Tighten the wing nut to secure the blade into position. Pull the veneer line through the jig, smoothly and in a straight line. Pass through other lines whilst the thicknesser is set to this position. Only a very small shaving of wood should be removed at each pass, so a gentle tap on the top of the blade should move it enough to shave the lines thinner still. Practise will give you the best idea of how much to tap the blade to give the best results.

SPARE VENEER LINES

Cut extra lines as it is not uncommon to break a few during the thinning process.

Inlay lines being brought down to the correct thickness with a purpose-built thicknesser.

Thickness dark lines a fraction thinner than light lines. When placed together darker lines can seem visually heavier, so if light lines are, for example, being scraped to 0.5mm, thickness dark lines to 0.4mm.

INLAYING THE SOUNDHOLE SURROUND

It is possible to inlay individual veneer lines directly into a routed trench in the soundboard, but this can be fraught with problems. Because the glue used to hold them together can swell the wood fibres slightly, you have to judge how loose or tight a fit the combined construction must be to allow for an ideal fit without having to resort to excess force to seat all of the lines. If they are not seated fully to the bottom of the trench you can also have the problem that, when the whole inlay is planed/scraped flush with the surface of the soundboard, some lines start to lose their definition and ugly gaps appear.

For these reasons alone, it is recommended that the inlays are fully constructed on jigs and are inlaid in one operation.

USING JIGS TO CONSTRUCT THE INLAYS

If the fingerboard is extended fully to the soundhole, and thereby covers up the top section of the soundhole surround inlay, then it is not necessary to make the inlay as a complete circle and therefore Jig A can be utilized. If, however, the fingerboard stops short of the soundhole, and the ring of the inlay can be seen in its entirety, then Jig B should be used.

Materials required for jig A

- The base: softwood (e.g. pine) 100mm (4in) *(L)* × 100mm (4in) *(W)* × 18mm (⁷⁄₁₀in) *(T)*;
- the disc: MDF measuring the inside diameter of the inlay ring × 6mm (¼in) *(T)*;
- dowel: 6mm (¼in);
- self-adhesive plastic;
- dressmaking pins.

This jig is made up of a softwood base topped with a disc of MDF, the diameter of which is the same as the *inside* diameter of the inlay ring.

First, cover the top face of the base with strips of self-adhesive plastic butted together to form a non-stick surface.

Drill a 6mm (¼in) hole through the centre of the base and mount the dowel in the hole.

Cut out the disc, the diameter of which should be the equivalent of the inside diameter of the inlay ring. Ensure that the disc is as round as possible and cover the edge with tape. Drill a 6mm (¼in) hole in the centre of the it and push the disc onto the dowel on the base.

Starting with the first *inner* veneer line, hold in position at the top point of the disc and pin in place. (Push the pin into the softwood base such that the side of the pin pushes the veneer line hard up against the side of the disc – do not pin through the veneer itself). Pull the line around the disc, pinning at regular intervals. Butt the end of the veneer line against the start end.

Paint a film of glue onto the first line, position the second line at the starting point and re-pin to hold both pieces against the disc. Pull the second line tightly around the first, re-pinning as you go and smoothing the pieces together with your finger. Ensure both lines are a snug fit, with no gaps between them. Also check that the lines are seated consistently on the base and have not risen up.

The soundhole inlay pinned together for Guitar #2.

GLUING THE INLAY LINES

Because the lines need holding together tightly, the glue used for this method was Original Titebond. Note that it is not essential that the line ends butt together precisely, as this section of the inlay will not be seen when assembled into the soundboard.

Repeat the above process with all of the remaining lines and allow the whole assembly to dry thoroughly.

Materials required for jig B

- The base: softwood (e.g. pine) 100mm (4in) *(L)* × 100mm (4in) *(W)* × 18mm (⁷⁄₁₀in) *(T)*;
- the plate: softwood (e.g. pine) 100mm (4in) *(L)* × 100mm (4in) *(W)* × 3mm (⅛in) *(T)*;
- self-adhesive plastic.

This jig is made up of a softwood base, topped with a thin plate of wood that has a hole cut out of it, the diameter of which is equivalent to the *outside* diameter of the inlay ring.

First, cover the top face of the base with strips of self-adhesive plastic butted together to form a non-stick surface.

Rout a hole in the centre of the plate, the diameter of which should be equivalent to the *outside* diameter of the inlay ring. Insulate the inside edge of the hole with tape or varnish to form a non-stick surface. Mount the plate onto the base and tape all round to hold both pieces securely together. Mark each quarter of the circle A, B, C and D.

Start with the first *outer* veneer line. Holding one end against point A, fit the veneer around the circle cut-out and mark with a pencil the other end overlong by 2mm (⁵⁄₆₄in). Remove the line and cut with a very sharp chisel at the pencil mark. Reapply the line, this time holding both ends together at point A, and gently push the remainder of the line around the hole's edge. This needs to be a tight fit, with no gaps or bagging. If it will not fit, remove the line, chisel a very small amount off one end and reapply. Repeat this process until the line fits tightly around the hole's edge.

SIZING THE VENEER LINES

Be aware that it takes an extremely small amount to make the difference between a too tight fit and a too loose fit.

Hold one end of the next veneer line against point B, fit the veneer line around the first line and mark with a pencil the other end overlong by 2mm (⁵⁄₆₄in). Remove the line and cut with a very sharp chisel at the pencil mark. Reapply the line, this time holding both ends together at point B, gently pushing the remainder of the line around the first line. This needs to be a tight fit, with no gaps or bagging. If it will not fit, remove it and chisel a very small amount off one end, then reapply. Repeat this process until the line fits tightly around the first line.

When you are satisfied with the fit, remove the second veneer line, apply a thin film of glue around face of the first veneer and remount the second veneer. Ensure that the bottom edges of both veneer lines are fully seated down onto the base.

Repeat for all of the remaining lines, staggering the joins around the jig each time.

FITTING THE VENEER LINES

- If each veneer line is fitted as tightly as possible, and the ends are staggered around the circle, you should end up with a soundhole surround that is gap-free and has invisible joins.
- If you wish to make one of the lines significantly wider than those bordering it, instead of trying to bend a thick piece use several thin pieces of the same wood to obtain the required width. Again, if the lines are fitted as tightly as possible any joins should be barely discernible.
- Because the lines are assembled very tightly, a glue thinner than Titebond Original can be used (for this example Super Phatic by Deluxe Materials).

When the whole assembly is thoroughly dry, lightly plane the surface to smooth and flatten. Turn out the assembly, reverse it and re-insert it into the jig, and then lightly plane the other side smooth and flat.

Routing the Inlay Trench

Cut a flat board (MDF or ply are ideal) at least the same size as the soundboard and drill a hole in it corresponding to the position of the soundhole centre, of a diameter suitable for locating the router base pin. The pin should be a snug fit so that there is no danger of it moving when in use.

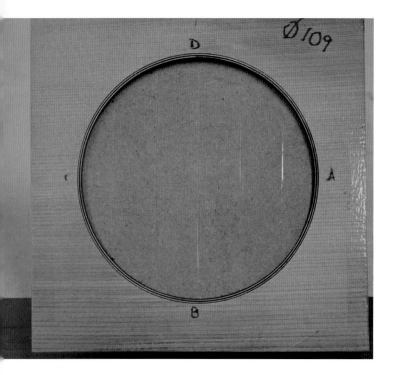

The inner soundhole inlay in the jig for Guitar #1.

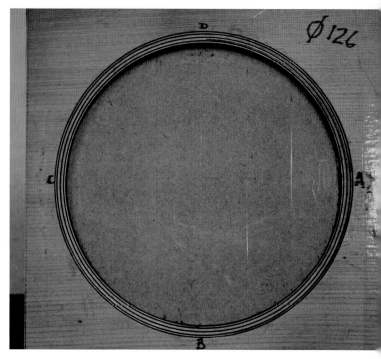

The middle soundhole inlay in the jig for Guitar #1.

The outer soundhole inlay in the jig for Guitar #1.

Mark with a sharp pencil the centre of the soundhole on the soundboard, directly on the centre join, along with the outer diameter of the soundhole and the inner and outer diameter of the inlay. Impress the centre mark with a bradawl and drill a hole at this point, the same diameter as that of the router base pin. Mount the soundboard over the pin on the flat mounting board and secure it to the board with clamps or tape around its edge.

TAKE CARE

Ensure any clamps or fixings do not impede the travel of the router.

Set the router such that the outer edge of the cutter is just shy of the mark denoting the outer diameter of the inlay, and rout a shallow trench (approximately 0.5mm deep) in a full circle. Offer up the inlay assembly to ascertain if the outer edge of the trench is correct for the outer diameter of the inlay. Adjust if necessary, and continue to rout the trench in small increments until the depth of the trench is half the thickness of the soundboard.

Routing the slots for the soundhole inlays on Guitar #1.

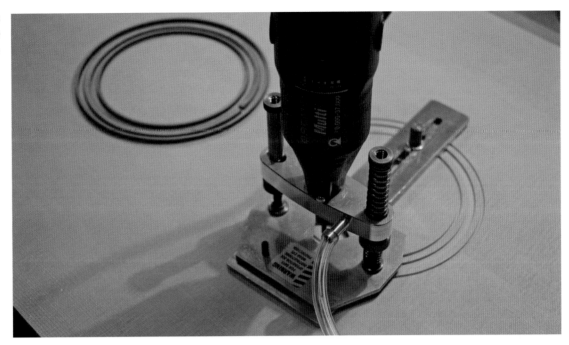

ACHIEVING A CLOSE FIT

For an ideal fit, the inlay needs to be a good snug fit into the routed trench. By initially routing slightly undersize, it is possible in subsequent passes to adjust the diameter minutely to obtain an accurate fit. If in doubt, practise this first on a scrap piece of soundboard.

Reset the router such that the outer edge of the cutter is just shy of the mark denoting the inner diameter of the inlay and rout a shallow trench in a full circle. Again offer up the inlay to determine closeness of fit and adjust if necessary. Rout to half the soundboard thickness. Rout out any remaining soundboard material between the two trenches to the same depth, so that the finished trench can accommodate the inlay.

GLUING THE INLAY

Applying glue will swell the wood fibres to some extent, so if the inlay is a very tight fit (if it has to be forced in with more than just finger pressure, for example) a small adjustment to the diameter of the trench may be necessary. Conversely, a loose fit will never look good, as this will result in unsightly gaps and ugly glue lines.

Apply glue to the soundboard trench and then push in the inlay firmly. Check that it is seated evenly all round, then place a wooden caul insulated with non-stick paper over the entire inlay and put a weight on top. Allow the glue to dry thoroughly.

Finally, plane or scrape the inlay flush with the soundboard's surface. Follow the circumference of the inlay carefully to avoid breakout of the inlay's edges. When level, lightly scrape the whole area to ensure the lines of the inlay are crisp and clean.

The Final Thickness of the Soundboard

Take this opportunity to adjust the final thickness of the soundboard to its optimum. Hold the soundboard lightly on either long edge with the flats of your hands and gently flop it up and down as if it was a piece of sheet metal. If there is no movement, then the soundboard is still too thick. Plane more off the thickness from the inside face of the soundboard and then retest. What you are looking for is a reasonable amount of movement, but not excessive flop as with a piece of card.

TESTING THE SOUNDBOARD THICKNESS

It takes some nerve to use this method to test the soundboard, as your first thought is that the glue joint will not stand this sort of treatment. It is in fact a good test of your planing and gluing, however, and if it fails now the chances are that it wouldn't have stood up to the rigours it would be subjected to in the future from string tension and so on.

Cutting the Soundhole

Replace the soundboard onto the router pin on the flat board and set up the router to the outside diameter of the soundhole. Secure the soundboard to the board to avoid any movement, as once the soundhole is cut right the way through it will have nothing to hold it steady.

Rout in shallow increments in three or four passes until the cutter breaks through the other side of the soundboard.

The Soundboard Braces and Tone Bars

Materials required

Note: All braces are made from quarter-sawn spruce. All of the major braces should be cut so that their lengths are sufficient to overlap the body profile by 6mm (¼in) (*see* below).

- S1 (X-brace arms): 420mm (16½in) *(L)* × 16mm (⅝in) *(H)* × 8mm (⁵⁄₁₆in) *(W)* with a 3mm arch (2 off);
- S2 (tone ars): 290mm (11⅜in) *(L)* × 14mm (⁹⁄₁₆in) *(H)* × 8mm (⁵⁄₁₆in) *(W)* with a 1.5mm arch (2 off);
- S3 (finger braces): 115mm (4½in) *(L)* × 8mm (⁵⁄₁₆in) *(H)* × 6mm (¼in) *(W)* with a very slight arch (2 off);
- S3 (finger braces): 100mm (4in) *(L)* × 8mm (⁵⁄₁₆in) *(H)* × 6mm (¼in) *(W)* with a very slight arch (2 off);
- S4 (soundhole reinforcement): 85mm (3⅜in) *(L)* × 8mm (⁵⁄₁₆in) *(H)* × 6mm (¼in) *(W)* with a very slight arch (2 off);
- S4 (soundhole reinforcement): 57mm (2¼in) *(L)* × 8mm (⁵⁄₁₆in) *(H)* × 6mm (¼in) *(W)* with a very slight arch (1 off);
- S5 (transverse brace): 280mm (11in) *(L)* × 20mm (²⁵⁄₃₂in) *(H)* × 16mm (⅝in) *(W)* with a 1.5mm arch (1 off);
- S6 (fingerboard patch): 203mm (8in) *(L)* × 3mm (⅛in) *(H)* × 25mm (1in) *(W)*, flat (1 off).

Ensuring the major braces are cut long enough to overlap the body profile is important for two reasons. First, it will ensure that any movement of the brace during the gluing process will still maintain sufficient additional length at the ends, and second, having protruding brace ends will greatly ease the fitting of the soundboard and the back to the ribs/**lining**s (*see* Chapter 4).

Plane each brace to the correct thickness. Utilizing the shooting/bench hook will greatly help this process. Plane one face flat and smooth, and then turn over and plane the opposite face flat and smooth, to a consistent and correct thickness.

Place the relevant template onto the brace, such that the centres of the brace and the template line up, and the arch is an equal distance in from the brace edge at each end. Draw the arch onto the brace and cut off the majority of the waste. It is very important that this arched edge is 90 degrees to the brace sides, so lay the brace onto the shooting board with the freshly cut curved edge overlapping the top section. With a sharp block plane on edge, smooth the curve to the line. Check that the edge is a consistent curve by placing it on a flat surface and rocking it from end to end. If it feels uneven and lumpy, it probably has flats or facets on it and will require further refining.

PLANING THE BRACE CURVE

It is preferable to plane the curve in long strokes from one end of the brace to the other, rather than in short cuts. Try to get a good flow going with the plane and then keep going until the line is reached.

If you have a corresponding **go-bar deck** dished board, the curve on the brace should match the curve on the **dished workboard**.

The Back

There seem to be two very different schools of thought as to how guitar backs perform and what they contribute to the production of sound. Some feel that the back should be stiff and inflexible, acting as a reflector of sound. Others feel that the back should be flexible and responsive, like the soundboard, to act in unison with it like a pair of bellows that pumps sound out of the soundhole. Whichever camp you subscribe to, bear in mind that the back should not be so thick that it adds a significant amount of weight to the instrument but conversely not too thin as to lose its constructional integrity.

Like the soundboard, the backs for the guitars being made here are thicknessed using a combination of tapping and flexing, with the ultimate aim of achieving a back that is relatively flexible, with a good ring to it, but not floppy. Although this will vary depending on wood species and even particular samples, the thickness arrived at is commonly around 2.5mm (1/10in).

Back Joining

Backs are supplied in two book-matched halves and are usually 5–6mm (1/4in) thick. These two halves require gluing together, which is best done whilst they are this thick. This allows for a small element of slippage: if the surfaces of each half become slightly misaligned during the gluing process it will still be possible to level them and have sufficient final thickness.

The procedures for shooting the back's edges, joining and then planing to thickness are the same as those for the soundboard described earlier in this chapter. You may also wish to insert a line or strip of purfling down the centre of the back. This can be simply done, by sandwiching a piece of inlay between the two halves of the back as they are joined together.

THE BACK JOIN REINFORCEMENT GRAFT

The inside of the back's join (or joins if multiple pieces are used to make up the width of the back) is strengthened by the **back graft**. This consists of strips of spruce or cedar, which are usually offcuts from the soundboard material. These should be cut so that the grain is running at right angles to the grain of the back, and across the join, not parallel to it.

Materials required
- Soundboard offcuts of sufficient length to span the gaps between the back braces + 3mm (1/8in) (L) × 12mm (1/2in) (W) × 2.5mm (1/10in) (T);

- a straight edge;
- a pencil;
- a wooden caul (long enough to span all of the offcuts);
- weights.

Mark around the body profile half template in pencil on the inside face of the back, ensuring that both halves match up perfectly either side of the centre line. Cut out the back to within 6mm (1/4in) of the line with a bandsaw or piercing saw.

Mark onto the inside face of the back the positions of all of its braces. Ensure that they are placed at 90 degrees to the centre line. It is only necessary to pencil in where the braces cross the outer profile line, and where they intersect with the centre reinforcement strip. Also mark the positions of the **tail block** and the neck block.

MARKING THE BRACE POSITIONS

This is best achieved by laying a straight edge along the centre line, marking the brace positions and then extending them from the centre with a set square resting on the straight edge.

Heavy pencil lines drawn across the whole width of the back can easily be mistaken for gaps between the brace and the back's surface. Conversely, a gap can look like a pencil line, so it is best to avoid this confusion by only marking where the braces cross the outer profile line and centre reinforcement strip.

Cut the soundboard offcuts sufficiently long to span the distance between the braces plus a little overlap, and also to run from the neck block to the first brace and the tail block to the last brace. Tape or clamp a straight edge half the width of the strips from the centre join and parallel to it.

Glue each offcut into position, butting up their edges against the straight edge, place a long wooden caul along the tops of the strips and place weights along its length. Alternatively, this can all be held in place in the go-bar deck. Allow the glue to dry thoroughly.

Round off the strip edges to create a gentle arch across their width. Trim back each offcut with a very sharp chisel exactly to the lines where the braces cross the centre join.

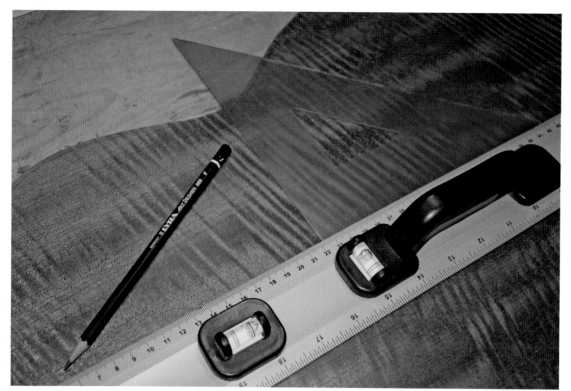

Marking the brace positions onto the back.

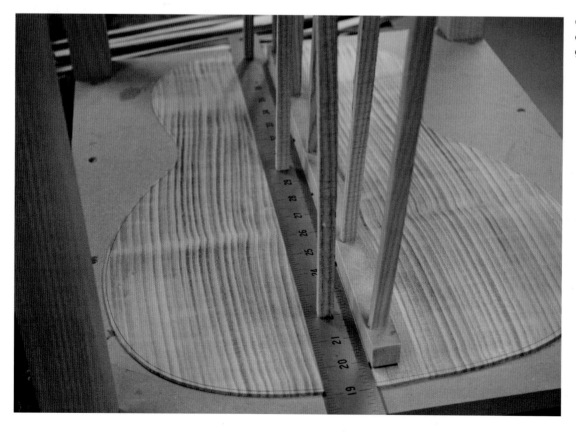

Gluing the back's centre graft in the go-bar deck.

The Back Braces

Materials required:

Note: All braces are made from quarter-sawn spruce, with the growth lines running vertically to the back's surface. All of the braces should be cut so that their lengths are sufficient to overlap the back profile by 6mm (¼in) (*see* below).

- B1 (upper bout brace): 280mm (11in) *(L)* × 16mm (⅝in) *(H)* × 9.5mm (⅜in) *(T)* with a 6mm arch (1 off);
- B2 (waist brace): 240mm (9½in) *(L)* × 16mm (⅝in) *(H)* × 9.5mm (⅜in) *(T)* with a 6mm arch (1 off);
- B3 (lower bout brace): 370mm (14½in) *(L)* × 16mm (⅝in) *(H)* × 9.5mm (⅜in) *(T)* with a 6mm arch (1 off);
- B4 (lower bout brace): 390mm (15⅜in) (L) × 16mm (⅝in) (H) × 9.5mm (⅜in) (T) with a 6mm arch (1 off).

CUTTING THE BRACES

If you are cutting the braces from a larger block, rough saw all braces over size in advance and stack on a shelf for as long as possible. When it is time to prepare them for use, only pick the ones that show no evidence of any major movement. If they are no longer straight and show a pronounced curve, discard them as they are not sufficiently stable.

Ensuring the braces are cut long enough to overlap the body profile is important for two reasons. First, it will ensure that any movement of the brace during the gluing process will still maintain sufficient additional length at the ends, and second, having protruding brace ends will greatly ease the fitting of the back to the ribs/linings (*see* Chapter 4).

Plane each brace to the correct thickness. Utilizing the shooting/bench hook will greatly help this process. Plane one face flat and smooth, and then turn over and plane the opposite face flat and smooth, to a consistent and correct thickness.

Place the relevant template onto the brace, such that the centres of the brace and the template line up and the arch is an equal distance in from the brace edge at each end. Draw the arch onto the brace and cut off the majority of the waste. It is very important that this arched edge is 90 degrees to the brace sides, so lay the brace onto the shooting board with the freshly cut curved edge overlapping the top section. With a sharp block plane on edge, smooth the curve to the line.

Check that the edge is a consistent curve by placing it on a flat surface and rocking it from end to end. If it feels uneven and lumpy, it probably has flats or facets on it and will require further refining.

PLANING THE BRACE CURVE

It is preferable to plane the curve in long strokes from one end of the brace to the other, rather than in short cuts. Try to get a good flow going with the plane and then keep going until the line is reached.

Planing the curve onto the bottom edge of a brace on a small shooting board.

If you have a corresponding go-bar deck dished board, the curve on the brace should match the curve on the dished board.

The Ribs/Sides

Materials and equipment required
- Book-matched rib blanks (2 off);
- a flat planing board;
- clamps;
- wooden cauls;
- a smoothing plane;
- a scraper plane.

It is important to plane the ribs to an even, consistent thickness, commonly 2mm (5/64in). If much thinner the ribs have a tendency to buckle when being heated for bending; if too thick then bending in a consistent curve is very much more difficult.

It is also vital to maintain a consistent thickness across the width of the rib. If it is thinner at one edge compared to the other it will bend at a different rate and produce an uneven profile.

Clamp the rib blank at one end to the flat board. Lightly plane smooth the majority of the face, then reverse the blank, and clamp and plane the remainder.

PLANING ADVICE

Always plane away from the clamp. If you plane towards the clamp along the rib's unsupported face and the plane blade digs in, the rib could buckle and very likely crack.

When the first face is smooth and flat, turn the blank over, clamp at one end and lightly smooth the other face in the same way. Repeat with the second rib.

Now is a good opportunity, whilst both blanks are smooth but over thick, to decide which of their faces is going to be the outside of the ribs. Ensure they are laid out as a matched pair, and mark on with a pencil the outside faces, left or right, and the top edge. It is very easy to forget or get confused which way round they should be, literally in the heat of the moment whilst bending, so this goes some way to alleviating the problem.

Thicknessing the mahogany ribs with a scraper plane.

Shoot the long edge on each rib that is designated as the soundboard edge, so that they are completely flat. Next reduce to the final thickness, planing the inside face of the ribs. This way, if there are any issues with grain tear-out and so on they will be on the inside. Having said that, however, you should strive to achieve as good a finish on the inside face as on the outside.

If you do experience the grain tearing due to figuring in the wood, revert to a sharp scraper to smooth to thickness.

Bending the Ribs

USING A BENDING IRON
To effectively bend a wooden rib to the guitar body's profile, it is necessary to heat the wood to make it pliable. The most commonly employed heat source is an electric bending iron. This consists of a shaped aluminium casting with a heating element embedded in its centre. The element heats the casting to a suitable temperature that is ideal for bending the rib.

TESTING THE TEMPERATURE

You can test if the iron is hot enough by letting a drop of water fall onto the top of the iron. If the droplet sizzles and jumps, the iron is up to temperature.

If you have never bent ribs before, it is a good idea to start with a practice rib, so that you can perfect your technique and avoid damaging the proper ribs due to inexperience.

The ribs need to be bent as true to the body profile as possible. As in the making of the rest of the guitar's components, it is bad practice to force a badly profiled part to fit, as this builds in unnecessary tension and could result in the failure of the component.

The ideal sequence is to start with the waist, to get this curve as good as you can get it. Then you can work out to the **upper bout** and then the **lower bout**.

Mark on the *outer* face of the rib the position of the waist and place this point against the hot iron. Warm either side of this point by rubbing the rib left and right until you feel the wood getting relatively pliable. Holding the rib either side of this point, apply gradual pressure to allow the rib to bend. Offer up the rib to the mould often, to ensure that you are bending to the true shape. When you are happy with the profile of the waist, turn the rib around and bend the upper and lower bouts with the *inner* face against the iron.

Once you are happy that the bent ribs follow the mould profile accurately, mount them into the mould and mark at each end where the centre line of the body lies. Cut the ribs just shy of this line.

Mount both ribs into the mould, soundboard edge downwards, so that they are flush with the bottom of the mould. Hold in place with turnbuckles or bent sticks.

GOOD PRACTICE ADVICE: BENDING THE RIBS (I)

- Keep the rib horizontal to ensure a consistent bend across the wood.
- Keep the rib moving – if it is held too long in one spot, it will scorch. On certain woods, like rosewood, this can dry out the wood so that it becomes brittle and will crack.
- If the wood you are using is reluctant to bend, you can help it by wiping the surface with a damp cloth. Subsequent application to the hot iron will then produce steam, which will help to soften the wood's fibres.
- Some particularly resistant woods (some rosewoods, for example) may require soaking before bending. However, in general try to avoid introducing too much water as this can cause the rib to buckle and distort.
- If a crack should occur (that is, a relatively minor one where the wood fibres separate from the surrounding area), reverse the rib and partially unbend it against the iron. Inject a small amount of glue under the fibres and then glue a piece of brown paper over the area to flatten and secure the raised shards. Allow this to dry and then recommence with the bending. The brown paper can be scraped off when the rib is fully bent. This is not always completely successful, depending on the severity of the crack, but it can often save a rib from being discarded.
- To check for consistent bending lay the bent rib on a flat surface, soundboard edge down, and, if bent right, this edge should touch the flat surface along its entire length. If this is not so, some re-bending is required. If you also hold the rib up and sight along from the lower bout, the upper bout should be parallel to it. Again, if this is not so, re-bend until the two line up.
- Don't overwork an area to try and get a bend exactly right (the lower bout is a relatively gentle curve, for example, and can be approximated quickly). In this way you can concentrate on achieving a consistent curve, whereas working on one spot for too long can create facets or flat spots. Once you have a good curve, you can then refine it to fit the template or mould.
- If you are using a highly figured wood for the ribs, there is a tendency for areas of figure (where the end grain rises to the surface of the wood) to crack, so employ a bending strap to aid the bending process. These are bendable steel strips with handles at each end. When placed parallel to and on the outside of the rib they help to hold and heat through the wood consistently, and lessen the chance of the wood cracking and checking (developing small surface cracks). If the wood is proving to be particularly difficult to bend, try placing a damp cloth between the bending strap and the rib whilst holding it to the iron.

Bending ribs on a hot iron using a bending strap
and a damp cloth.

Cutaway rib installed – note the spruce corner block.

TAKE CARE

*Do not over tighten turnbuckles, as this can distort
the mould and significantly alter the width of the
instrument's body.*

Cutaway Models

If your guitar is going to have a cutaway, the rib on that side
should be bent to conform to the body contour and also to
the cutaway.

THE VENETIAN CUTAWAY

This is the cutaway type that is rounded and continuous
(that is, where the lower bout, waist and the upper bout
that includes the cutaway are made from one continuous
piece of rib). To aid the bending of the tight curves of the
cutaway it is quite acceptable to thin the rib in this area to
1.5mm (¹⁄₁₆in).

GOOD PRACTICE ADVICE:
BENDING THE RIBS (II)

- Ribs will bend easiest if they do not include excessive
  waste wood across their width. Therefore, it is recommended that ribs are cut to a width just over the
  maximum depth of the guitar (minus the thickness
  of the back and soundboard).
- It is possible to cut the rear arch onto the back edge
  of the ribs, but this can have its disadvantages. It
  can be confusing whilst bending as to which edge
  you have uppermost, and consequently whether
  you should hold the rib horizontal to that edge. It
  is better to make a clear acetate template that can
  be wrapped around the fully bent sides to mark on
  the arch. This has the added advantage that you can
  more accurately match each rib.
- If the guitar is going to have a cutaway, pre-profiling
  the rib will give the cutaway's curved section the
  wrong height (it will be too low in the centre).
  Remember that the back is arched from front to
  back and side to side, so as the cutaway curves
  back into the body area, its centre needs to be at a
  greater height than its ends.

THE FLORENTINE CUTAWAY

This is the cutaway type that is pointed and is made up of more than one piece. In this case the lower bout, the waist and the area up to the cutaway are made from one continuous piece of rib. The cutaway itself is a separate piece, bent to its curve and joined to the main rib with a mitre joint, and reinforced with a corner block. Again, to aid the bending of the tight curve of this piece it is quite acceptable to thin it to 1.5mm (¹⁄₁₆in).

The Neck and Tail Blocks

The Neck Block

This block is very important, as it anchors the neck to the body. It therefore has to be substantial enough to withstand the quite considerable string tension. On a steel string guitar, this block is invariably separate from the neck (as opposed to the integral slipper heel block found on classical guitars) and is commonly made from a light but strong wood such as mahogany.

There is some debate as to the ideal orientation of the grain of this block. If the grain runs horizontally, in common with the grain of the ribs, there is a danger that any cracks or splits occurring in the sides could continue through the block also. However, one advantage of this orientation is that the top and bottom of the block is side grain, and therefore it is much easier to shape and offers up a better gluing surface to the soundboard and back.

If the grain runs vertically, this helps to overcome the likelihood of splits continuing unopposed. The disadvantage of this orientation is that the soundboard and back are glued to end grain, which is not as good a gluing surface as side grain.

GRAIN DIRECTION

Remember the general rule that two pieces of wood glued together are strongest if the wood grain of each piece is at right angles to each other.

The neck and tail blocks on the guitars shown here are constructed from three separate pieces, the major piece having vertical grain, with caps top- and bottom-orientated so that their grain is horizontal, thereby achieving a compromise between the two options discussed.

Materials and equipment required

- Mahogany: 43mm (1¹¹⁄₁₆in) *(L)* × 75mm (3in) *(W)* × 35mm (1⅜in) *(T)* (1 off);
- mahogany: 75mm (3in) *(L)* × 35mm (1⅜in) *(W)* × 20mm (²⁵⁄₃₂in) *(T)* (2 off);
- mahogany (tenon): 25mm (1in) *(L)* × 75mm (3in) *(W)* × 6mm (¼in) *(T)* (1 off);
- a router table;
- a 6mm (¼in) router cutter.

Prepare all pieces so that they are completely flat and square, especially the end grain faces of the main block. Set up the router table fence such that the cutter is halfway across the thickness of the block. Mark the face of the block that will run along the fence as the datum face.

Rout a slot 6mm (¼in) deep across both ends of the main block and rout a similar slot across one face of each end piece. Cut two pieces of the tenon 12mm (½in) long. Glue each piece into the slots of the main block, then add glue to protruding tenon and end grain of the block and assemble the end pieces, clamping across the whole assembly. Allow to dry thoroughly.

A laminated neck block blank.

The neck block being installed, clamped to the top bout rib and sideways to the cutaway rib.

The Tail Block

Materials and equipment required

- Mahogany: 60mm (2¹¹⁄₃₂in) *(L)* × 80mm (3⅛in) *(W)* × 25mm (1in) *(T)* (1 off);
- Mahogany: 80mm (3⅛in) *(L)* × 25mm (1in) *(W)* × 20mm (²⁵⁄₃₂in) *(T)* (2 off);
- mahogany (tenon): 25mm (1in) *(L)* × 80mm (3⅛in) *(W)* × 6mm (¼in) *(T)* (1 off);
- a router table;
- a 6mm (¼in) router cutter.

Prepare the timber, rout the slots and glue the whole assembly together as per the neck block described previously.

Shaping the Blocks

The faces of the neck and tail block that will be glued to the ribs require shaping to the profile of the body at these areas. If the guitar you are working on has a flat profile where the neck joins the body, as on many larger steel string guitars, then this face should be planed flat. However, the 000 guitars detailed in this book have a curved profile and the blocks should be shaped to fit this curve exactly. Regularly offer up the block to the mould whilst shaping to check for a good fit.

PREPARING THE BLOCK FACES

It is very important that the block's face is flat and straight from top to bottom and square to the top (soundboard) end. This can be ascertained by checking with an engineer's square. This is especially important for the neck block, as any irregularity can render neck fitting difficult and can seriously impair the neck join geometry.

If you are making a guitar with a cutaway, the side of the block has to be contoured to the cutaway's profile, and again to the top face it should be straight and flat from top to bottom and square.

Installing the Blocks

Align the flat top edge of the ribs with the mould's face and clamp in position. With the mould face downwards, raise the whole mould up 1–2mm by sliding thin laths under the face.

Offer up the neck block, align the centre lines and clamp in place. Check one last time for a good fit before removing the clamps, applying glue to the contoured face of the block and re-clamping into place.

Repeat the described procedure with the tail block.

Allow the glue to dry thoroughly and then plane the top/
soundboard faces of the blocks flush with the ribs/surface of
the mould.

Shaping the Back Curve onto the Ribs

Lay an acetate template of the side profile inside each rib in
turn, and mark the back arch onto the inside face of each rib.
Cut away the majority of the excess wood with a chisel, being
careful to pare shavings and not to cut away too much at a
time. Then refine with a block plane, trimming to the line. If
done properly, you can plane a continuous edge free of lumps
and dips.

The ribs should end up sloping very gradually from the
tail block to the waist, and then dip gently down to the neck
block. A good way to ensure that this is a gradual curve, and
not pointed or facetted, is to lay a large flat board onto the
ribs and rock it forwards and backwards between the tail
block and the neck block. It should rock consistently and not
in a series of jerky movements (which would indicate flats on
the rib edges).

The Linings

To increase the gluing area for the soundboard perimeter,
and without adding a significant amount of weight to the
ribs, it is necessary to glue a narrow lining around the top and
bottom edge of the ribs. These linings can be solid, but most
commonly they are strips of wood that have been almost
sawn through at regular intervals to make them very flexible.
They are invariably made from mahogany and are known as
'kerfed' linings. It is best if they can be glued on in a continuous strip, to strengthen and maintain the symmetry of the
rib's curves.

The linings need to be held securely at regular and frequent
intervals whilst they are being glued. Good clamps can be

Kerfed lining being glued and clamped to cutaway – note the
slope of the neck block formed to accept the
curve of the back.

made from clothes pegs with the grip enhanced by wrapping
rubber bands around them, or you can use spring clamps as
used on the guitars here.

The kerfed linings used here are a standard type, with the
continuous face being glued against the ribs. It is possible to
obtain 'reverse kerfed' linings, where the cut faces are glued
against the ribs. This type is deemed to add more stiffness
to the ribs and a better, smoother look to the inside of the
instrument. However, due to their added stiffness they are
prone to break easily, so it is recommended that they are
dampened and bent to shape and allowed to dry before
assembling.

As always, do a dry run first before applying any glue. Start
to lay a length of lining from one side of the neck block,
clamping as you go. The lining should just sit proud of the rib
edge. When you are satisfied that this is so for the complete
length from neck to tail block, unclamp half of the lining,
paint glue onto the lining's face, then reattach and re-clamp.
Repeat with the other side.

Gluing on the kerfed linings using spring clamps.

FITTING THE LININGS

For the back linings, it may be necessary to cut through the linings partially to enable them to follow the curve of the ribs. It will be necessary to push the rib assembly partially through the mould to access and clamp linings to the straight (soundboard) edge of the ribs.

When the glue is dry, plane the top edge of the linings flush with the edge of the ribs. Whilst making the linings flush with the rib edges that will accommodate the back, tilt the plane slightly downward to the outside so that the resultant edge has a shallow angle. This is necessary as the back will be domed and consequently its edge will not attach to the ribs/linings on a level plane. For this reason also, the back edge of the tail block should have an angle planed onto it to receive the curved back. The back edge of the neck block should also be angled to receive the back without making it dip unnaturally.

Clamping on rib-strengthener strips under a wooden caul.

Rib-strengthening Strips

As previously discussed, if a rib does develop any cracks lengthways over time (not uncommon on rosewood or mahogany guitars) and these are left unchecked, they can increase in length to such a point as to seriously compromise the guitar body's structure. This can be alleviated to some degree by gluing light but strong wooden strips across the ribs at several points around its profile.

Inside Guitar #1, showing the rib-strengthener strips, cutaway corner block and kerfed linings.

The End Graft

Where the two ribs butt together at the tail block, it has to be decided whether they will join together as an exact fitting seam or, as more commonly executed, with an inlay dividing the two halves. An inlay, or **end graft**, could be as simple as a single line or group of contrasting lines or, as in this case, a block of wood flanked by purfling strips.

If fitting a block this is invariably tapered, wide at the top and narrowing toward the back. In this way, you can achieve a good, tight fit.

Materials required
- A piece of ebony/rosewood (1 off); and strips of purfling (2 off).

Secure the rib assembly such that the tail is facing upwards (carefully clamping the tail block in a vice is one way of achieving this). Re-establish the centre line of the tail block and mark it onto the top and bottom of the ribs. Mark out the desired graft taper, measuring either side of the centre line to ensure the inlay will be centralized.

Hold a straight edge along these lines and score them with a very sharp marking knife. Go over the lines several times, cutting deeper at each pass, ensuring that the cut is vertical. Stop when you are satisfied that the cut is the thickness of the ribs (2mm or 5⁄64in). Chisel out the waste rib to achieve a flat-bottomed, vertical-walled trench. Cut the block (ebony, in this case) to the exact same taper, but overlong at the top and

Materials required
- Lengths of quarter-sawn spruce: 95mm (3¾in) *(L)* × 6mm (¼in) *(W)* × 2.5mm (¹⁄₁₀in) *(T)* (8 off).

Lightly bevel the edges of these strips. Cut them to length such that each strip fits snugly between the top and bottom linings. Glue and clamp them into place, using a wooden caul to spread the pressure.

The tail graft inlay with purfling lines ready to be glued in.

The tail graft glued in.

bottom. Slide the graft into the cut-out and determine a snug fit. If it is not, trim the sides of the graft until its fit is gap-free and tight. If purfling is going to be fitted, these can be slid in either side of the graft.

Apply glue to the trench, slide in all pieces until tightly fitting and leave to dry. Plane the assembly flush to the contour of the body profile and then trim the top and bottom overhang of the graft flush with the edges of the ribs.

The Neck Joint Mortice

The neck joint on the guitars described in this book will employ a mortice and tenon (*see* 'The Neck Joint' section in Chapter 5 for further explanation). It is advisable to cut the mortice into the neck block at this stage (before the back and soundboard are attached).

Mark onto the top of the neck block a mortice slot 20mm ($^{13}/_{16}$in) deep by 20mm ($^{13}/_{16}$in) wide. Ensure that the width is equidistant either side of the centre line – 10mm ($^{13}/_{32}$in) either side – and parallel to it. Continue the lines down the front of the neck block and then mark the slot outline on the bottom face of the block. Score around all of the pencil marks with a sharp marking knife to clearly and accurately define the outline of the mortice slot outline.

The mortice slot cut out of the neck block.

Cut down into the slot either side with a hand saw or bandsaw, just shy of the scored line, and then carefully chisel out the bulk of the waste wood. Pare the remainder to the line, being careful not to go beyond it, checking regularly that the back and the sides of the slot are flat and square.

The neck mortice marked out and scored on the neck block.

The Truss Rod Adjustment Access Hole

Ascertain the position of the truss rod adjuster and mark this onto the centre of the back wall of the neck mortice slot.

ALLOWANCE FOR THE SOUNDBOARD

Remember to allow for the thickness of the soundboard, which will eventually be glued to the top of the neck block. The top surface of the soundboard will be flush with the top of the neck.

Drill a pilot hole through the block, being sure that the drill is at 90 degrees to the block and parallel to the centre line of the body. Drill most of the way through from the outside face with the correct size drill bit and then complete the hole from the inside. This will ensure that the drill bit does not break out the inside face and leave a ragged hole. Lightly countersink both ends of the hole to neaten them up.

The truss rod adjustment hole drilled into the neck block.

Shaping the Neck and Tail Block

The sharp corners of the neck and tail blocks can be bevelled or rounded off, which relieves the blocks of a bit of weight without compromising their strength. These corners can either be planed or chiselled off and then smoothed down.

CHAPTER FOUR

ASSEMBLING THE COMPONENT PARTS OF THE BODY

Unless the workshop that you have been working in and in which your materials are being stored maintains a constant atmosphere, it is best to assemble the guitar's components in a relatively quick manner. This should avoid the possibility of a fully braced back or soundboard being left for a long length of time, vulnerable to excessive movement due to fluctuating humidity. It is not unheard of for a brace with a 6mm (¼in) convex arch to revert to a concave one if left long enough in an area that is subject to extreme humidity levels (*see* 'A Note From the Author' for a possible cure).

Assembly 1: Completing the Back

Gluing on the Bracing

If using a go-bar deck, place the back centrally on the 6mm (¼in) dished workboard. Place the braces in position one at a time and secure with go-bars, one at each end of the brace and one in the centre. If necessary add two more bars equally spaced along the length of the brace. If there are any gaps then the brace arch needs more work but if the brace fits the curve precisely, remove the bars, run a bead of glue along the brace's curved edge, reposition and ensure the brace ends overlap the profile evenly, and re-secure with bars. Repeat with the other braces until they are all installed. Allow the glue to dry thoroughly.

OPPOSITE PAGE:
Guitar #2: The rib and back assembly clamped into its mould.

Gluing the braces to the back in the go-bar deck.

PLACING THE GO-BARS

When placing the initial go-bar, there can be a tendency for the brace to slide out of line. Install a second bar promptly, bent the opposite way to equalize the pressure.

Profiling the Braces

Place the back onto a firm surface and place blocks or wedges around the perimeter to keep it stable and secure. Clean off any glue squeeze-out with a very sharp chisel by paring down carefully using the brace's side as a guide, and also towards the base of the brace using the backs surface as a guide, and with the chisel's bevel downwards. Be extra careful not to remove any wood in the process.

The brace ends require carving down to a much lower height, which will allow the back's perimeter a degree of flexibility when assembled to the ribs. This is known as scalloping and is achieved by utilizing a chisel with the bevel down and paring down in a gentle curve such that the brace ends at the back's profile are 2.5mm (⅒in) high.

With a block plane placed on its edge, the sides of the brace should then be shaped in carefully towards the centre of the brace, creating a rounded peak. Ensure you protect the surface of the back from damage from the plane's edges by utilizing tape or a piece of card or aeroply secured to the back.

Clean up all the internal surfaces either with a scraper or fine abrasive to remove all tool marks, glue residue and so on.

Assembly 2: Gluing the Back to the Ribs

Fitting the Back

Place the mould top-face down onto a flat surface and ensure that the top (soundboard) edges of the ribs are also seated flush onto the flat surface.

Offer up the back with an equal amount of overlap all round and with the centre line of the back corresponding to the centre line of the mould. Hold it in place by lightly clamping or taping it to stop the back from moving.

With a pencil, mark onto the outside of the ribs the precise positions of the protruding brace ends. It is also necessary to mark onto the brace ends the point where they cross the outside of the ribs. Remove the back.

Continue the brace end markings across the top edge of the kerfed linings. With a fine saw, cut down at an angle along these lines, being careful not to cut into the rib. With a narrow chisel, excavate a pocket in the lining, to a depth that matches the height of the brace ends – in this case 2.5mm (⅒in). Score around the pocket regularly with a sharp scalpel to define its outline and to enable whole shavings to be removed to leave a neat, vertically walled recess.

Kerfed linings notched to accommodate the brace ends.

A back brace housed into kerfed lining.

The protruding ends of the braces can now be cut back so that they stop short of the perimeter profile line by the thickness of the ribs, in this case 2mm (5⁄64in). Measure this distance in from the pencilled lines and trim to this point.

The majority of the excess brace end can be partially cut through with a fine saw, being careful not to mar the surface of the back. The rest should then be cut away carefully with a chisel. Cut just shy of the line on the brace, offer up the back to the ribs and check for a snug fit into the linings. If the braces are still overlong then trim them back by paring down the ends, taking only very fine shavings with a chisel, again being very careful not to damage the back.

Spool Clamps

It is recommended that spool clamps are used to aid the gluing of the soundboard and the back to the ribs. They can be bought but are easy to make, which will save you quite a lot of money. You will require approximately forty of these very simple clamps, which can be used repeatedly over your making career.

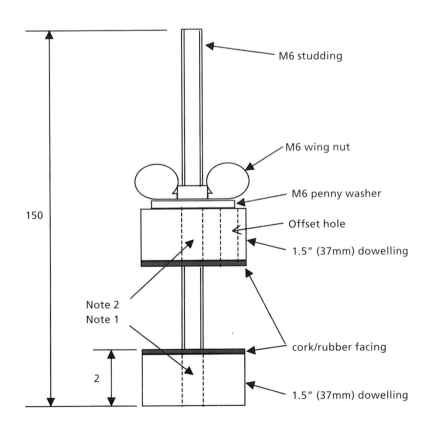

Spool clamp design.

Notes
1. Drill 6mm hole in bottom dowelling and glue studding in.
2. Drill two 7mm clearance holes in top dowelling.
3. All dimensions are approximate.
4. You will require around forty clamps for the average sized instrument.

Parts list (for forty clamps):
• Lengths of M6 studding.
• 2m of 37mm diameter dowelling (perhaps a broom handle).
• Forty M6 wing nuts (40 off).
• Forty M6 penny washers (40 off).
• Cork or rubber facing.
• Araldite for gluing studding.
• Appropriate glue for fixing cork/rubber.

89

Spool clamps ready to swing round and clamp back to the ribs.

Gluing the Back

Assemble the spool clamps, one in each hole around the perimeter of the mould, so that the fixed spool is flush with the front of the mould and with the top (soundboard) edge of the ribs. Run a nut down the threaded rod of each clamp to hold it in place. Thread a loose spool onto the threaded rod via its offset hole, followed by its washer and wing nut, and swing out of the way.

Re-attach the back, swing the loose spool on each clamp over the perimeter of the back and tighten its wing nut. For the neck and tail block, place a clamping caul on each of these areas and hold down using wooden cam clamps. Check one last time that the back fits to the ribs and is free of gaps.

If there are no gaps displace the clamps spools, remove the back and run a bead of glue along the rib edges and the

The back of Guitar #1 being glued onto the ribs.

The back graft trimmed back to butt up against the tail block.

tops of the linings, and across the tail and neck block ends. Re-attach the back and tighten down all of the clamps as per the dry run. Allow the glue to dry thoroughly.

GLUE RECOMMENDATION

Titebond supply a version of their original glue known as Extend. This has a longer opening time so is ideal for this application to allow time to spread the glue, assemble the back and tighten down each clamp.

Now reverse the mould and place it down on a padded surface. As the back has got an arch, place blocks or wedges around the perimeter to stabilize the assembly and keep it level.

Clean up any glue squeeze-out from fitting the back and take this opportunity to scrupulously clean the entire interior of the assembly of any glue spots, rough edges and other imperfections.

Fitting a Maker's Label

Maker's labels are your opportunity to advertise your wares, and they traditionally include the maker's name, the year

and place of manufacture, and possibly a serial number. It is debatable whether they should be affixed so that they are readable whilst the instrument is in an upright position (perhaps hanging on a wall in a shop waiting for the right customer to come along), or whilst in the playing position (readable by an eager punter who simply must rush out and buy one of your instruments). The decision is yours!

Maker's label affixed and lined up with the centre of the soundhole.

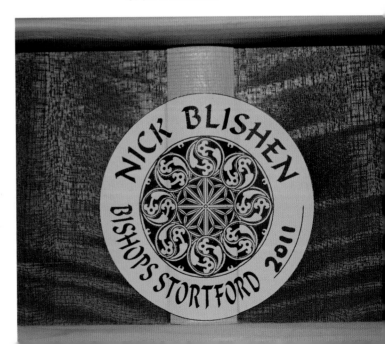

Assembly 3: Completing the Soundboard

The steel-string soundboard has a number of braces and struts glued across its internal face. The braces have to perform two very different tasks. They are placed to strengthen the soundboard in such a way as to resist approximately 84kg (185lb) of constant string tension. They also have to allow the top to vibrate and produce a resonant tone. If the braces are too heavy and stiff, the soundboard will have very strong structural integrity but it will sound dead and unresponsive. If the braces are flimsy and overly flexible, the tone can be very indeterminate and the top will be in danger of buckling and caving in. A solution for a happy medium has to be found. Luthiers often expound on the theory that the best guitars are the ones just on the point of collapse – but the trick is reaching that goal without going too far.

The components required for this part of the assembly are as follows:

Fingerboard patch   This is glued on flat.

Transverse bar   This has a 1.5mm (¹⁄₁₆in) arch planed onto its gluing edge.

Soundhole braces   These have a very small arch planed onto their gluing edges.

X-Brace   The arms have a 3mm (¹⁄₈in) arch planed onto their gluing edges.

Finger braces   These have a 1.5mm (¹⁄₁₆in) arch planed onto their gluing edge.

Tone bars   These have a 1.5mm (¹⁄₁₆in) arch planed onto their gluing edge.

Laying Out the Bracing

Mark around the body profile half template in pencil on the inside face of the soundboard, ensuring that both halves match up perfectly either side of the centre line. Cut out the soundboard to within 5mm (³⁄₁₆in) of the line with a bandsaw or piercing saw.

THE FINGERBOARD PATCH
Place the soundboard centrally onto the *flat* side of the workboard in the go-bar deck and glue the fingerboard patch into its correct position. Allow to dry thoroughly.

Soundhole strengthening braces being glued on in the go-bar deck.

A temporary end stop taped to the soundboard to prevent the fingerboard patch from sliding.

PREVENTING SLIPPAGE

Once glue is applied, the patch will want to slide about during clamping. Small corner templates, cut from scraps of aeroply taped temporarily to the soundboard, will help to keep the patch in place.

THE X-BRACE ASSEMBLY

It is very convenient to make a full-size cardboard template of the complete soundboard and to draw onto it all of the braces in their correct positions. The points at which the braces cross the body profile can be denoted by cutting notches into the card with a sharp knife. Intersections and centre lines can also be cut out so that these points can be transferred to the inside face of the soundboard proper. The other reason for having this template is to be able to lay out the soundboard braces, most importantly the X-brace arms, to determine their exact intersection.

Place the template onto a level surface that is raised up sufficiently to enable clamps to be positioned around its perimeter. Lay one arm of the X-brace onto its corresponding position on the template, slide appropriately sized wedges under the brace ends and clamp in place. Place the second arm of the X-brace following its corresponding position, lying over the first arm, and clamp in place with appropriately sized wedges under the brace ends. The intersection where the two brace arms cross needs to be accurately marked by scoring with a knife.

THE X-BRACE INTERSECTION

The X-brace intersection is not normally at 90 degrees, so it is vital that the join is cut to the correct angle.

The two arms are joined together using what is known as a half lap joint, that is, a notch is cut in the underside of the top arm halfway up its height and to a width corresponding to the thickness of the lower brace, and a notch is cut in the topside of the lower arm halfway down its height and to a width corresponding to the thickness of the upper brace.

Mark a point on each side of each X-brace arm measuring half the arm's height. Using an engineer's square, continue the scored intersection lines to these points. Cut out the notches with a fine saw, just shy of the lines, to remove the majority of the waste. With a very sharp chisel, pare away the remaining waste to the lines, taking off very fine shavings. Test for a snug fit regularly so that you don't over-enlarge the notches, which will result in a sloppy fit. The aim is for a good close fit that will not move once assembled, but not so tight that it could result in the wood splitting.

This join is often reinforced with a glued-on patch or section of cotton tape, but for added strength the braces described here are inlaid with a thin plate of maple on the top and underneath of the assembly to form a more continuous construction. To this end, a 1mm (³⁄₆₄in) × 20mm (²⁵⁄₃₂in) long recess is cut either side of each brace's notch.

Apply glue to the notches, assemble the two arms and then hold them together on the go-bar deck's 3mm (⅛in) dished workboard whilst drying.

KEEP YOUR WORKBOARD CLEAN

Place a baking or greaseproof sheet under the X-brace join to protect the workboard from any glue squeeze-out. (An ideal material is made by DuPont™ – a Teflon®-coated non-stick cooking mat, which is a thin, flexible sheet.)

Make two hardwood inlays the exact width of the braces and length of the recess, but 2.5mm (¹⁄₁₀in) thick. Glue and clamp both into place and allow the glue to dry thoroughly. Level the inlays, ensuring they maintain the smooth curve of the braces.

If, as on the soundboard described here, the tone bars are to be inset into the X-brace arms then place the X-brace assembly back onto the card template and secure into place. Place the tone bars into position and mark onto the X-brace arm exactly where the bars touch. Unclamp and remove the assembly and then notch the arm to allow for the tone bar ends to be housed snugly.

Gluing on the Bracing

Place the soundboard centrally onto the 3mm dished workboard in the go-bar deck, position the X brace and hold down with go-bars. Check that there are no gaps between the brace arms and the surface of the soundboard. Remove the brace assembly, apply a bead of glue along both arms, re-apply and re-clamp with the go-bars.

Place the tone bars in position, again holding them down with go-bars. If satisfied that the fit is gap-free, then glue in place. Repeat for all braces.

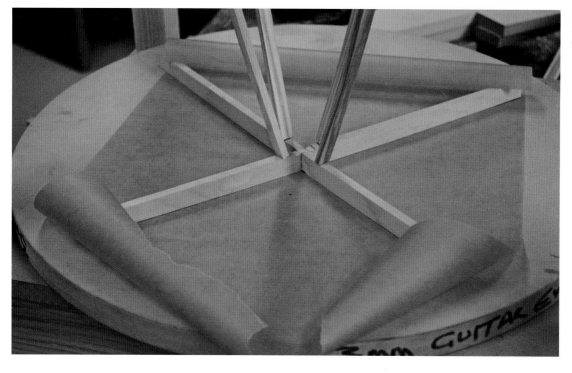

Gluing the X-brace arms together in the go-bar deck.

The soundboard braces being glued on in the go-bar deck.

The finger braces being glued on in the go-bar deck.

WORKING EFFICIENTLY

Work from the centremost braces outwards. If you are careful, and do not disturb the go-bars already in position, all braces can be assembled and glued in one operation.

Lastly, trim the sides of the **bridge plate** to fit precisely between the X-brace arms and with the front edge positioned in the correct place. Fashion a wooden caul the same shape as the plate to distribute the clamping pressure, apply glue and then clamp the bridge plate into place.

The bridge plate being glued on in the go-bar deck.

Profiling the Braces

Place the soundboard on a firm surface and place blocks or wedges around the perimeter to keep it stable and secure. Clean off any glue squeeze-out with a very sharp chisel by paring down carefully using the brace's side as a guide, and also towards the base of the brace using the soundboard surface as a guide, with the chisel's bevel downwards. Be extra careful not to remove any wood in the process.

The lower arms of the X brace should be scooped from just beyond the intersection to within 75mm (3in) of the end, at which point the brace is 12.5mm (½in) high. The brace

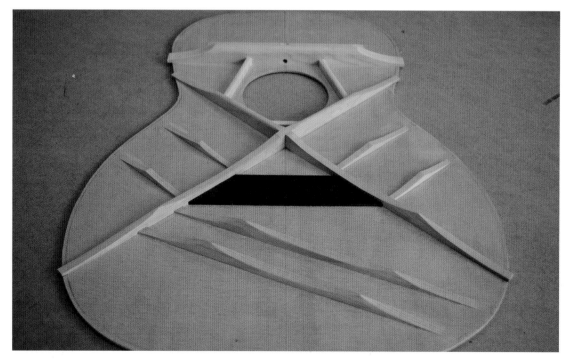

The soundboard for Guitar #2 (right-handed) with fully shaped and scalloped braces.

The soundboard for Guitar #1 (left-handed) with fully shaped and scalloped braces.

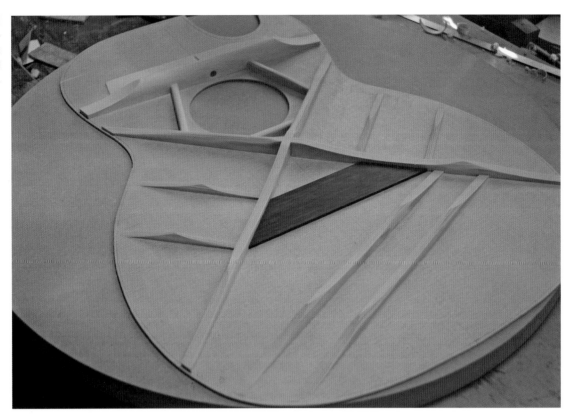

should then be scalloped down to 2.5mm (¹⁄₁₀in) high. Then shape the high points in towards the centre of the brace, creating a rounded peak.

The upper arms should be gently ramped down to within 75mm (3in) of the end, at which point the brace is 12.5mm (½in) high. The brace should then be scalloped down to 2.5mm (¹⁄₁₀in) high. These ends will be located into the kerfed lining on the ribs. The sharp top edges of the braces need to be rounded off. This has to be done in part with a sharp chisel as the layout of the braces does not allow access to a plane. Hold each end of one of the X-brace arms and try and flex the soundboard. If there is no movement, then scoop a little more wood out of the lower arm. It should be able to flex by about 1.5mm (¹⁄₁₆in). Repeat with the other X-brace arm.

The tone bars require a similar treatment, although they will stop short of the linings by 3mm (⅛in).

The upper transverse brace should be scalloped at each end and will locate into the linings. The top edges require rounding off, but it is left fairly substantial and inflexible.

The finger braces also need to be shaped, peaking roughly in the middle of their length and stopping short of the linings by 3mm (⅛in).

The fingerboard patch should have any sharp corners rounded off, as should the soundhole braces.

Finally, clean up all of the internal surfaces with either a scraper or fine abrasive to remove all tool marks, glue residue and so on.

Reinforcement Cleats

If the guitar you are building is going to be kept in a part of the country that suffers from wildly varying extremes of humidity, it may be well worth reinforcing the vulnerable part of the soundboard join below the bridge area. **Cleats** are very small, thin squares of quarter-sawn spruce (soundboard offcuts are ideal) that are glued across the underside of the soundboard across its join. The grain direction of the cleats should run at 90 degrees to the grain of the soundboard for maximum strength.

Cut the cleats 10mm (¹³⁄₃₂in) square and 2mm (⁵⁄₆₄in) thick. Glue one between the bridge plate and the first tone bar, one between the two tone bars and one between the second tone bar and the tail block area. When the glue has dried thoroughly on all cleats, their weight can be lightened further by carefully carving down from the centre of the cleat to each side, forming a pyramid-shaped top surface. If the cleats are too substantial, they can affect the soundboards vibrations, so they must be kept as light as possible.

Assembly 4: Gluing the Soundboard to the Ribs

Fitting and Gluing the Soundboard

Check that the ribs/linings are flush and that the entire top of the profile is flat. Push the assembly up through the mould

so that there is approximately 25mm (1in) protruding above the surface.

Offer up the soundboard with an equal amount of overlap all round and with the centre line of the soundboard corresponding to the centre line of the mould. Hold it in place by lightly clamping or taping it to prevent it from moving.

With a pencil, mark onto the outside of the ribs the precise positions of the protruding brace ends. It is also necessary to mark onto the brace ends the point at which they cross the outside of the ribs. Remove the soundboard.

Mark and cut out the brace end pockets as for the fitting of the back described previously for Assembly 2. Trim the brace ends until a good fit is achieved.

The rib assembly can be removed from the mould, as gluing on the back should have locked the body shape sufficiently to make further use of the mould unnecessary.

The kerfed linings notched out to house the brace ends.

The soundboard for Guitar #1 being glued on.

Assemble the soundboard onto the rib assembly. Hold the head and tail ends with cam clamps utilizing clamping cauls to spread the pressure and with spool clamps at regular intervals around the perimeter. Check one last time that the fit is gap-free and that centre lines correspond. When you are happy that all is well, remove the clamps and soundboard, run glue around the perimeter, re-attach the soundboard and re-clamp. Allow to dry thoroughly.

Trimming Flush the Back and Soundboard Overhang

With a sharp chisel or spokeshave, trim the back's excess overhang carefully until it is almost flush with the ribs. Revert to a scraper and then trim back until the back is perfectly flush with the ribs. Repeat this procedure with the soundboard overhang.

TAKE CARE

As the soundboard is a softwood, its edge has a tendency to tear and chip, so do not be tempted to cut away more than fine shavings. Also, as it is composed of alternating hard and soft annual growth lines, it can be hard to smooth flush. It may be necessary to achieve this with the help of a small fine file.

The mortice slot bottom block being glued in.

The Mortice Slot Bottom Block

Cut a piece of mahogany that fits the neck mortice slot width-ways, but approximately 12.5mm (½in) high and slightly oversized from front to back. Glue this in to the bottom of the slot and when dry trim it flush to the rib outline. This acts as a depth stop for the neck tenon when the neck is installed.

Binding/Purfling

The binding (a border line of wood or plastic) that is inlaid around the perimeter of the body is functional as well as decorative. It helps to protect the vulnerable edge of the soundboard and also seals the end grain of the front and back, thus making them less prone to the absorption or loss of moisture due to extremes of humidity.

Purfling is a line, or group of lines, of inlay between the binding and the front or the back that is mostly decorative, although it is usually only applied to the soundboard face of the instrument.

Binding is commonly made from a contrasting material and creates a definitive border. It is a matter of taste as to the colour of the binding, but generally dark materials are used against pale soundboards like spruce and light ones are used against dark wood like rosewood or ebony. What is best avoided is a light wood directly adjoining another light-coloured wood, as unless the join is perfect any irregularities show up as ugly glue lines.

The material used is also a matter of taste. Plastic binding can be bought pre-sized and is relatively easy to install, although it is recommended that it is glued on with a suitable cement. For the guitars here, ebony binding is used on Guitar #1 (to match the ebony fingerboard, headstock veneer and the bridge) and rosewood is used on Guitar #2 (for the same reasons). For Guitar #1 it has also been decided to install four lines of purfling (white/black/white/black) to complement the soundhole surround inlay. It is a personal preference, but after the enormous lengths gone to when choosing appropriate timbers, careful inlays and so on, it seems a bit cheap to fit plastic bindings.

CUTTING THE LEDGE FOR THE BINDING AND PURFLING

For the binding, a ledge needs to be cut around the perimeter of the body, to the same depth as the thickness of the ribs (in this case 2mm or ⁵⁄₆₄in) and to a height to accommodate virtually the full height of the binding. It is preferable to end up with the binding being slightly proud of the ledge so that it can be trimmed down flush after gluing. The bindings used on the guitars here are 2.5mm (¹⁄₁₀in) × 6mm (¼in), so a ledge 2mm (⁵⁄₆₄in) × 5.5mm (⁷⁄₃₂in) was cut to accommodate them.

There are several ways to mark out the ledge. A traditional way is to utilize a tool known as a purfling marker. This is only used to score a line to denote the height and depth of the trench (*see* 'Tools' section in Chapter 1), but generally the body of the marker is run around the ribs as a guide and a knife blade scores a line parallel to the ribs.

Scoring with a knife blade has to be done gradually and with some patience, as there is a danger that the blade will veer off course if you try to cut too deep. It is best to score lightly all round, and then repeat, cutting deeper still. Once a clearly defined line is evident, it is recommended that you revert to a sharp knife like a scalpel held vertically, to cut deeper.

The height of the ledge is scored by running the purfling marker's body around the soundboard's face for the top binding and the back's face for the rear binding. The scored lines should then be cut deeper with a scalpel. Pare away the waste carefully with a very sharp chisel.

CUT WITH PRECISION

It is very important that the resultant ledge is consistent, square and with a sharp corner.

To cut a ledge for any purfling the marker is again run around the ribs, this time with the cutter set for the inside edge of the purfling and to cut to half the soundboard's thickness. For Guitar #1 the combined depth of the four lines was 2.0mm (³⁄₃₂in), so they were set into the soundboard in a ledge measuring 2.0mm (³⁄₃₂in) wide × 1.5mm (¹⁄₁₆in) deep.

Using a router
Even if you are using a router to cut the ledge, it is advantageous to first score lines denoting its depth and height. Set the purfling marker to the required setting (commonly 2mm or ⁵⁄₆₄in for the depth, 5mm or ³⁄₁₆in for the height) and run the marker against the ribs, scoring a light line around the whole body profile. Don't try to score too deep, as this can distort the blade and send it off course. Go around several times, each time cutting a little deeper, until there is a clearly defined line. Then revert to using a sharp knife like a scalpel and cut the line deeper still.

Scoring a line around the body profile with a purfling marker.

The scored line being made deeper with a scalpel.

Cutting out the binding channel with a chisel.

The fully excavated binding channel.

The binding and purfling channel around the cutaway on Guitar #1.

TAKE CARE

If using a router, ensure that a block of wood is inserted into the neck block's mortice slot, to prevent the router from running into and cutting off course as it passes this point.

It is recommended that the purfling marker is loaded with a #15 scalpel blade. This has a curved end and tends not to stick or snag in the scored line. Angle it slightly back from the vertical. The scalpel handle used here is loaded with a #10A scalpel blade. This has a pointed end and tends to cut deeper without going off track.

The binding channel being cut out with a Dremel router.

The binding and purfling channel around the tail block on Guitar #1.

When routing the channel for the back, bear in mind the fact that the back plate has a pronounced arch. Because of this, if you try to rout using the ribs and back to guide the router, the curved back will tip the router slightly off the perpendicular. It is possible to excavate most of the trench in this way, but it is better to finish off with a chisel.

Inlaying the Purfling

If the purflings used are a pre-made combination of lines – a chevron or herringbone pattern, for example – they need to be bent precisely to the purfling channel profile using a hot bending iron. It may be necessary to dampen the purfling to soften the fibres, but be careful not to over-soak them as they may delaminate.

The purfling fitted to Guitar #1 is made up of individual lines that are thin enough to bend without heating and are best glued in individually. The method used is similar to that employed for making the soundhole inlay; that is, lines are glued into the channel and held in place by vertical pins inserted into the soft spruce of the soundboard.

Start at the neck block end and work around to the tail. With a small artist's brush, apply glue to the initial 100mm (4in) of the first line, place it into the purfling channel and hold it in place with vertical pins. Make sure that the side of the pin is tight against the purfling line and not piercing it. Run your finger firmly around the line to ensure a good gap-free fit. Apply glue to the next few inches and pin the subsequent section in a similar manner.

Continue until you reach the tail, where the line can be trimmed just beyond the centre line. Apply glue to the initial 100mm (4in) of the second line and place it into the purfling channel hard up against the first line. Run your finger

A purfling line glued and held in place with pins.

A purfling line glued and held in place with pins up to the cutaway.

firmly around the line to ensure a good gap-free fit and re-pin to hold the purfling lines in place. Apply glue to the next few inches and pin the subsequent section in a similar manner. Continue until you reach the tail, where the line can be trimmed just beyond the centre line. When all lines are installed, leave it to allow the glue to dry. Then, very carefully, trim back all of the lines to the centre line.

Repeat the above procedure on the second half, but this time start at the tail, making sure that all new lines butt up against the lines from the first half. Allow the glue to dry thoroughly.

Bending Wooden Binding

Two lengths of binding are generally employed for both the front and the back, joining at the tail of the body. These bindings require bending as accurately to the body profile as possible. Wooden bindings benefit from being soaked for an hour prior to bending to help soften the wood fibres.

TAKE CARE

Ebony bindings are prone to cracking, so bend them slowly and patiently. With care it is possible to end up with four bindings, but allow for a couple of spares if disaster strikes.

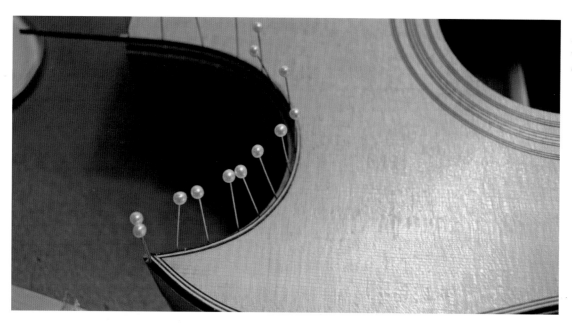

Purfling lines glued and held in place with pins around cutaway.

A water trough for soaking bindings prior to bending.

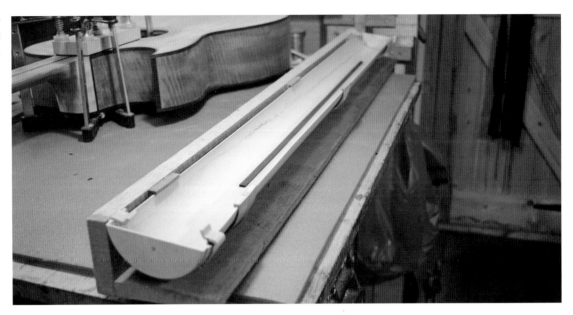

Bending an ebony binding on a hot iron.

Ebony and rosewood binding clamped into the mould for safe storage before using.

Bindings are bent in the same way as the ribs, starting at the waist and then moving out to the upper and lower bouts. Offer them up to the body profile regularly to determine a good close fit.

It is good practice to bend all of the binding needed for the jobs in hand, and to store them clamped into the mould until they are needed for the gluing process.

Once you are satisfied that the binding profile is accurate, the bindings need to be glued into the ledge. Do a dry run first, noting any areas where the binding does not fit tightly into the depth of the ledge or is not seated properly into the height. Adjust where necessary.

CHECKING FOR SQUARENESS

Check that the bottom edge of the binding is still square to its sides. It sometimes happens that during the bending process the wood distorts sufficiently to render this edge no longer perpendicular. This must be corrected, as the binding will then not seat into the channel snugly and will leave gaps. Either run the binding over a sanding board or carefully level it with a block plane.

An efficient method is needed for holding the binding into the ledge while the glue is drying. It is possible to achieve this by using long rubber bands, or even by wrapping the whole assembly with tyre inner tubes. However, these methods take some practise and involve quick assembly (both halves of the binding can be installed at the same time using these methods). A slightly more sedate, and less stressful way, is to use masking tape. As a lot of these tapes have a bit of stretch to them, they are ideal for pulling the binding into the ledges.

Cut several lengths of tape, and line them up along the front of the bench for easy access. Starting from the neck block, apply glue with a small artist's brush to a section of the ledge, then slot in the binding and tape into place. Alternate each piece of tape such that one is stuck first to the soundboard and pulled over the binding and stretched down and the other end stuck to the rib. The next piece of tape should be first stuck to the rib and pulled up over the binding and stretched over and stuck to the soundboard. In this way, the combined pull of the alternate pieces of tape help to seat the binding to the side of the soundboard and also down to the bottom of the ledge.

Apply further glue to the next section of the ledge and tape the binding into place. Repeat the steps described until the binding is glued and taped around the lower bout and heading for the tail block. Hold the binding in place and mark on it the point where it crosses the centre line. Place a block of scrap wood next to the tail and at the same height, rest the end of the binding onto it and cut just beyond this mark. If there is a relatively large amount of excess length, cut it back with a fine razor saw. Carefully pare back with a very sharp chisel, cutting at 45 degrees (the angle facing inwards to the soundboard) until this bevel is centred on the body centre line. Glue and tape into place.

Repeat the above for the second half of the binding until it approaches the first half at the tail block. Hold the last length into place and mark where it crosses the centre line, and cut just beyond this mark. Carefully pare back with a very sharp chisel, cutting at 45 degrees (the angle facing outward from the soundboard) until you can locate this half precisely into the bevel of the first. Glue and tape the final section, and allow the whole assembly to dry thoroughly.

TAKE CARE

Be careful when removing the tape, as it can pull up shards of wood from the soundboard. Pull the tape diagonally and slowly to prevent this.

The body binding glued and taped on.

The body binding ends being cut to form a tight scarf joint.

The scarfed join of binding.

Removing tape slowly at an angle to avoid pulling up the wood grain.

The body binding glued and taped on up to the cutaway.

The body binding glued and taped around cutaway.

Binding awaiting gluing in at the neck end of the cutaway.

The cutaway binding being levelled flush with a curved scraper.

The binding at the cutaway point being levelled flush with a curved scraper.

The ribs trimmed back to allow the binding of the point of the cutaway.

Alternative binding for the cutaway point: two pieces glued together or one solid piece.

Binding the Back

This process is a repeat of the one for binding the sound-board, described above.

Trimming the Binding and Purfling Flush

Invariably, the binding and the purfling will sit proud of the ribs or soundboard, so they need to be brought down flush with them. For this purpose, it is best to use a very sharp scraper to remove any excess. A new Stanley knife blade used as a scraper is ideal for bringing purflings down level.

Scraping bindings flush with the ribs.

CHAPTER FIVE

ASSEMBLING THE NECK, FINGERBOARD AND FRETTING

Fitting the Neck

The Neck Joint

A good neck joint is vital for stability, tone transference, longevity and so on. A traditional neck joint on steel-string guitars is the dovetail. This is very strong and efficient, but is very difficult to get right. An alternative method is to cut a mortice and tenon joint, which is either glued or bolted in.

The guitars described here employ a method that is a combination of several techniques, and therefore much easier to get right (thanks to Norman Myall for the 'neck joint without tears' separate tenon method, and also the late, great Irving Sloane for the pseudo dovetail dowelling method).

The main problem with dovetail or fixed tenon joints is that the necks on steel-string guitars do not attach to the body on a horizontal plane. Generally these necks are installed angled back from the right angle by approximately 1–1.5 degrees (*see* 'The Correct Neck Angle' for a full explanation).

The Separate Neck Tenon

Cut a piece of good quality hardwood (in this case maple) to 22mm (⅞in) × 22mm (⅞in) × 76mm (3in) long and plane this down to fit the mortice slot. This should initially be a good snug fit, so that it will hold in place whilst shaping. The outside face of the block must match the external contour of the ribs precisely, especially if the body profile is curved at this point. Carefully plane this face of the tenon so that it is

OPPOSITE PAGE:
Guitar #1: The neck being fitted to the body.

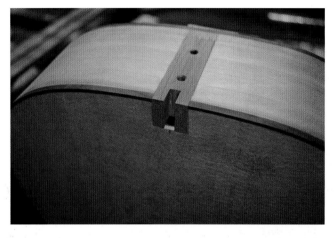

A separate tenon block fashioned to fit the mortice slot, complete with screw holes and truss rod adjustment slot.

continuous with the ribs and the whole neck heel area is flat across the depth of the ribs (from soundboard to back).

Mark a centre line down the inside back face of the tenon and drill two countersunk holes through from this face of the block that will accept No.8 countersunk screws. Next, run a saw down the centre line to create a shallow notch; this will help when assembling the neck, as it will allow excess glue to flow into it. Cut a slot in the top of the block that matches the truss rod slot in the neck.

The Correct Neck Angle

As previously discussed, invariably the neck does not join to the body on a horizontal plane, but is set back by approximately 1–1.5 degrees. To determine the exact angle, it is best to make a few measurements to ensure good geometry.

One method is to calculate three separate heights at which you want the string path to be from the neck to the **saddle**. When all three points line up then the neck should be at its ideal angle. Here is an example of this measuring method:

Point #1: At the nut   The height of the bottom of the string above the surface of the neck will be the thickness of the fingerboard plus the height of the first fret (the bottom of the nut string slots are virtually level with the top of the first fret).
   e.g. 6mm (0.24in) + 1mm (0.04in) = ***7mm (0.28in)***

Point #2: At the twelfth fret   The height of the bottom of the string above the surface of the neck will be the thickness of the fingerboard plus the height of the twelfth fret plus the ideal string height at the twelfth fret.
   e.g. 6mm (0.24in) + 1mm (0.04in) + 2.5mm (0.1in) = ***9.5mm (0.38in)***

The neck centre line being aligned with body centre line.

FITTING THE NECK HEEL TO THE BODY

If you are finding it difficult to ascertain if the heel is fitting the body precisely, scribble chalk over the area on the body where the heel will join and then rub the neck heel in small back-and-forth movements just over this area. Inspect the back face of the heel and notice to where the chalk has transferred. These patches are going to be points where the two surfaces touch – so conversely areas with no chalk are points where the two surfaces *do not* touch. Lightly shave off the areas that have chalk on them and repeat the rubbing process until chalk transfer covers the whole area.

   An alternative method is to tape a piece of abrasive over the area on the body where the heel will join and then rub the neck heel in small back-and-forth movements just over this area. Be very careful if using this method, however, as it is very easy to round off edges, which can result in an even worse fit.

Point #3: At the bridge saddle   The height of the bottom of the string above the surface of the soundboard at the spot where the centre of the bridge saddle will be at an ideal bridge and saddle height.
   e.g. Bridge at 10mm (0.39in) + saddle at 2mm (0.08in) = ***12mm (0.47in)***
   Cut three blocks of wood 7mm (0.28in) high, 9.5mm (0.38in) high and 12.7mm (0.47in) high and temporarily affix them in their respective positions (at the nut, twelfth fret and saddle position) with double-sided tape.

   Offer up the neck to the body (a strap clamp is a good way to hold the neck in position) and lay a long straight edge such that it spans the false nut position to the block representing the bridge saddle. If the straight edge is not touching the twelfth fret position block, then the neck is angled too far forward and the back of the heel needs to be shaved to a more acute angle. Alternatively, if the straight edge is resting on the twelfth fret position block but is not touching the saddle position block, the neck is angled too far back and the back of the heel needs to be re-profiled to a shallower angle. The back of the heel needs to be altered until the straight edge sits perfectly on all three blocks.

   It is also very important to ensure the following.

- The back of the heel must sit precisely against the body without any gaps at all. If the body profile is

✳ 12.00 mm

curved at the neck position, an identical curve must be fashioned onto the back of the heel. It is also vital that the front shaped face of the tenon touches the back of the heel along its length.

- The neck must retain its geometry with respect to its centre line. Place a long straight edge aligned along the centre line of the body and ensure that the centre line of the neck lies on its path.

Fixing the Tenon to the Neck

If, as advised, the tenon is a tight fit, remove it and take a fine shaving off the width. Re-check that the tenon is a good fit: not loose, but not so tight that it is difficult to pull out.

When you are satisfied that the neck fits the body precisely (that is, the angle at which the two join is correct for an ideal string height and action, and the centre lines correspond), then the tenon needs to be glued to the back of the heel. Initially, this is only temporarily affixed. Apply two *very small* dots of glue to the front edge of the tenon, locate the neck and hold it in place with a strap clamp. Check that the alignment is still correct and leave the glue to dry thoroughly.

Remove the neck along with the tenon and drill through the two screw holes in the tenon with the same size drill bit, just enough to indent the back of the heel. This should help to centralize a pilot drill, which should be slightly smaller than the diameters of the screws designated to be used. Drill these pilot holes just deep enough to accommodate the screw's lengths. Be careful not to drill any deeper than necessary, especially at the bottom of the heel where it tapers to a shallower thickness. Insert the two screws and tighten home fully.

Remove the screws and remove the tenon by giving it a smart tap with a mallet via a short length of timber. Apply sufficient glue to the surface of the tenon, reattach it to the heel and screw into place. Once dry, again remove the screws, drill out the screw holes with an appropriate bit and glue in dowels in their place.

If all of the above is done correctly it should be possible to attach the neck to the body, and it should line up correctly.

The Dowelling Method

Assemble the neck to the body and strap clamp it into place. Drill 10mm ($1^3/_{32}$in) holes either side of the tenon, half into the

A drilling jig for the neck tenon dowels.

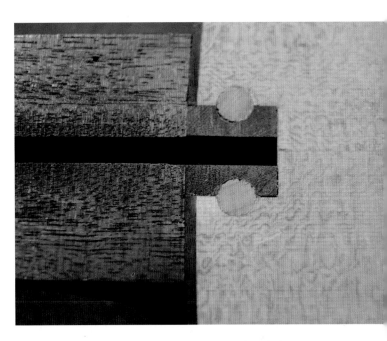

The neck tenon dowels glued in and levelled.

tenon and half into the neck block, deep enough to accept a 10mm ($1^3/_{32}$in) dowel. A simple wooden jig can be made to ensure that the holes are vertical and equidistant.

Remove the neck and glue a dowel into each half-hole recess on either side of the tenon. When the neck is reassembled to the body, these dowels will lock the joint together.

SPRAY FINISHING

If the guitar is going to be spray finished, it can be done at this stage, whilst the body and neck are separate. This avoids any build-up of finish around the heel area.

All gluing surface areas on the tenon and mortice slot need to be masked to keep them as bare wood. It is also necessary to mask off the area of the bridge (see Chapter 6).

Carefully remove any squeeze-out from gluing in the dowels and check the neck alignment one more time. If correct, apply glue to the tenon, then reassemble and clamp into place.

The guitar body being held by large rubber bands in a purpose-made cradle.

GLUING THE MORTICE AND TENON

If the mortice and tenon joint is a tight fit, it may be problematic reinserting the tenon fully once the glue is applied. For this reason, it would be advantageous to ensure that the fit is a relatively easy one (not sloppy) and to use only sufficient glue to wet the mating surface. Cutting a notch down the back of the tenon can also help by allowing any excess glue to flow into it.

Installing the Truss Rod

The method depends on the type of truss rod used, but the two-way rod here is simply placed into the neck slot, with the adjuster to the bottom of the slot, and aligned with the hole in the neck block. A half hardwood dowel should then be glued in the slot at the headstock end for one end of the truss rod to bear against.

A thin film of silicon needs to be spread along the bottom of the trench before the rod is installed. This will ensure both that the truss rod does not rattle and, as the silicon never goes fully hard, that the rod can still be adjusted when necessary.

Glue a hardwood block into the top of the tenon slot to retain the truss rod, being careful that no glue is allowed to foul the working of the adjuster screw.

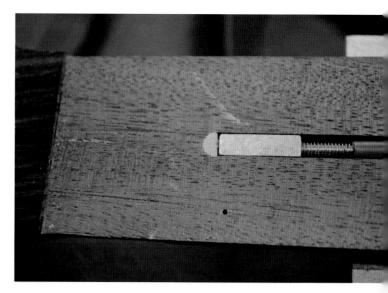

Half of a hardwood dowel glued into the slot against which one end of the truss rod can bear.

The truss rod inserted and the block to retain it glued in.

The Heel Cap

Heel caps finish off the bottom of the heel. They are made here from the same woods as the bindings.

Fashion a slightly oversized piece of wood for the heel cap and profile its back edge so that it fits the contour of the body precisely. Glue and clamp in place, and allow to dry thoroughly. Trim back to the heel profile so that it blends in.

The heel cap being glued and clamped on.

The Fingerboard and Its Frets

A Brief History

THE FRETS

Old guitars of the Renaissance and baroque periods used gut strings, often in paired courses, either tuned in unison with each other or an octave apart. This was in common with lutes and vihuelas, as was the tradition of utilizing loops of gut tied round the neck to form frets. The manufacture and quality of gut strings of the time was relatively inconsistent, so much so that players often had trouble with intonation between adjacent courses of strings. Because the frets were tied on and moveable, however, they could be repositioned or slanted across the fingerboards to adjust for these inconsistencies. The fact that pressing gut strings onto gut frets produced relatively little wear also meant that this arrangement lasted for quite some time.

However, as players clamoured for a greater range (baroque guitars commonly had only five courses and lacked the sixth or equivalent lowest note of the modern guitar) manufacturers experimented with and introduced wound strings (which were initially silk thread wound with silver wire). This enabled makers to introduce six course/string instruments, but the downside was that the wound strings wore the gut frets very quickly. An alternative was therefore sought and fixed frets of a harder material (ebony or strips of brass) were used. These evolved into the type of profile common today, which takes the form of a domed head with a barbed tang running underneath that is inlaid into the fingerboard.

FRET POSITIONING

The positioning of frets on stringed instruments was determined by Vincenzo Galileo as long ago as 1581. His formula used the ratio of 18:17 to locate frets for any scale length, which is virtually equivalent to the Equal Tempered Scale that is used to this day. This is often referred to as the 'Rule of Eighteen', where the first fret was established by dividing the overall string length – the length of the string from the bridge saddle to the nut (dimension 1) – by eighteen, and the resultant number was the measurement from the nut to the centre of the first fret. This measurement was then subtracted from dimension 1 to give a figure for a new string length (dimension 2), which represented the measurement from the bridge saddle to the first fret. Dimension 2 was then divided by eighteen, and the resultant number was the measurement from the first fret to the second fret. This measurement was then subtracted from dimension 2 to give a figure for a new string length (dimension 3), which represented the measurement from the bridge saddle to the second fret. This process was repeated until all the remaining fret positions were established.

This method was initially more than adequate, especially as the frets were moveable and could be adjusted for small alterations in intonation. As string manufacture became more consistent, and wound strings for the lower courses were introduced, tied on gut frets were replaced by fixed ones and the formula to establish their positions was refined from using 18 to 17.817. This method can be used to determine the fret positions for any string length.

Another method that will give identical results is to divide the string length (dimension 1) by 1.059463. This will give the distance from the saddle to the first fret (dimension 2). This distance can then in turn be divided by 1.059463 to give the distance from the saddle to the second fret (dimension 3).

For example, for an instrument with a string length of 650mm (25.59in):

Distance from saddle to centre of first fret:	650 ÷ 1.059463 = 613.518358
Distance from saddle to centre of second fret:	613.518358 ÷ 1.059463 = 579.08426
Distance from saddle to centre of third fret:	579.08426 ÷ 1.059463 = 546.5828

MEASURING FRET DISTANCES

The most accurate method of ascertaining all of the fret positions is with a calculator, keeping the number of decimal places as calculated. However, in practice it is impossible to mark the fret positions to the resultant accuracy. When you have calculated all of the positions, round each measurement up or down to one decimal point.

It is far more reliable to measure each fret position from one point, either the saddle or the nut. If measurements are taken from fret to fret, and one of the dimensions is incorrect, then that will throw all of the frets that follow out of alignment.

The scale length for the guitars featured here is 643.6mm (25.34in), a standard Martin-style string length. The calculations for this length, measured from the saddle, are as follows:

0. 643.6mm (25.34in)
1. 607.5mm (23.92in)
2. 573.4mm (22.57in)
3. 541.2mm (21.31in)
4. 510.8mm (20.11in)
5. 482.1mm (18.98in)
6. 455.1mm (17.92in)
7. 429.5mm (16.91in)
8. 405.4mm (15.96in)
9. 382.7mm (15.07in)
10. 361.2mm (14.22in)
11. 340.9mm (13.42in)
12. 321.8mm (12.67in)
13. 303.7mm (11.96in)
14. 286.7mm (11.29in)
15. 270.6mm (10.65in)
16. 255.4mm (10.06in)
17. 241.0mm (9.49in)
18. 227.5mm (8.96in)
19. 214.7mm (8.45in)
20. 202.7mm (7.98in)

Making the Fingerboard

Fingerboards need to be made from a durable hardwood, as they will have to stand up to heavy wear from having metal strings pressed down onto them. For this reason, the most common timbers used are rosewood and ebony. This is not to say that other woods cannot be used, but for longevity these two are deemed best suited for this purpose.

As they are such hard woods, planing them flat and to size takes time, patience and very sharp blades. Be prepared to resharpen more than once to achieve a good blemish-free surface. As always, an extremely sharp plane set for very fine shavings will give the best results.

Flatten and smooth one face of the timber and repeat on the other face, ensuring a consistent thickness. If you have an oblong fingerboard blank, plane one long edge flat and square to the face. This will be the datum edge. If the fingerboard blank is already tapered along its length then draw on a centre line, mark the exact taper of the neck you are using and plane the sides of the fingerboard blank to these lines.

Cutting the Fret Slots

This must be done very accurately, to ensure that the frets are in their correct positions for good intonation.

An ebony fingerboard blank being planed flat and to the
correct thickness with a block plane.

The ideal slot is one that is the same width as the **fret
tang** of the wire being used and is marginally deeper than
the tang's height. This will ensure that the fret is well seated
into the slot with no excessive airspace and that it is held
in by the tang's barbs. The slots must also be vertical to
allow the crown of the fret to sit level with the surface of the
fingerboard.

Place a long rule along the fingerboard blank on its centre
line, with the overall string length measurement placed
precisely on the end that denotes the front of the nut. For
example, if the string length is 650mm (25.59in), place the
rule such that the 650mm mark on the rule is at the nut end of
the blank. Clamp or tape the rule into place so that it cannot
move. Then read back from this measurement at each fret
position and mark with a scalpel on the centre line.

OBLONG FINGERBOARD BLANKS

On an oblong fingerboard, place an engineer's square on
the datum edge and scribe the fret position lines right across
the blank in each position. The slots can now be cut with the
appropriate saw (with a blade kerf width the same as that of
the fret tang) using the engineer's square as a guide to starting the saw cut. Take your time, concentrating on keeping the
cut vertical and square.

Some specialist fret saws have depth stops supplied with
them, but a simple one can be made from a thin piece of
wood clamped to the blade, with its long edge the right distance from the saw's teeth. This also helps to stiffen the saw
blade, which is normally very thin and consequently over-
flexible. Check that the slots are deep enough along their
whole length. This is done easily with a piece of thin card
with a line drawn on it denoting the required depth. Drag it
through the slot and if the line appears above the surface of
the fingerboard then it is not deep enough at that point.

CUTTING THE FRET SLOTS TO DEPTH

*It is best not to greatly exceed the slot depth, as this
can weaken the fingerboard and consequently affect the
overall stiffness of the neck. However, it is important that
slots are deep enough so that frets can be seated fully
against the fingerboard's surface.*

TAPERED FINGERBOARD BLANKS

Because tapered fingerboard blanks do not provide a straight
edge against which to measure, a way has to be found to
enable the cutting of the fret slots square to the fingerboard's

A fret slot cutting jig (this is a mandolin version, but it is
relevant to any fretted fingerboard).

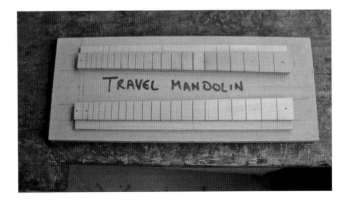

centre line. The simple jig illustrated here re-establishes a datum edge parallel to the centre line to allow the marking and sawing the slots with the aid of an engineer's square as described above. This jig also has the advantage that once made it can be used again to make further fingerboards of the same size and scale length.

BOUND FINGERBOARDS

Some fingerboards are bound, that is, they have an edge or binding around their perimeter, sometimes in a contrasting wood or material. Not only is this decorative, but it also serves to cover the ends of the fret slots.

Guitar #1 has a bound fingerboard, with ebony binding and several lines of purfling. (Ebony binding is used here as it matches the body binding and the purfling of maple/ebony/maple.)

The fingerboard taper should be cut so that the overall size is minus the thickness of the binding, in this case 1.5mm (1⁄16in), and the thickness of the purfling if used, in this case 1.5mm (1⁄16in). The binding and purfling run across the soundboard end of the fingerboard and up each side to the nut end. The joins where the pieces meet are mitred. The three purfling lines were stuck together first, to ease the mitring and joining process.

Cover the bottom face of the fingerboard fully with two or three layers of masking tape. This will raise the board up sufficiently from the workboard whilst the purfling is affixed to its sides and ensure that when the purfling and binding is glued on, there is no danger of it rising higher than the bottom edge of the main fingerboard blank. The whole assembly can then be planed flush after the binding has been completed.

Cut both of the side purfling pieces overlong and glue them to the sides of the tapered fingerboard blank. The same jig that is used for joining the soundboard and back halves together was employed for this operation (see Chapter 4). A piece of straight thick perspex was used between the wedges and the fingerboard assembly to spread the clamping load. Allow to dry thoroughly.

The fingerboard can be fixed to a workboard to prevent it moving whilst you are working. It can be held in place by utilizing the two pin holes in frets one and eleven (see page 123). Push a panel pin through these pilot holes so that they make an impression in the workboard. Drill these impressions approximately 6mm (¼in) deep, making sure that they are vertical. Crop the heads off two pins that are long enough to be able to be pushed into these holes with approximately

3mm (1⁄8in) of the pointed end sticking up above the surface. Locate the fingerboard carefully onto these two pins and push it down onto the board.

Cut the end piece of purfling overlong and lay it in place at the end of the fingerboard and on top of the protruding side purfling pieces. Mark the thickness of the end piece onto the side pieces and then trim it back with a very sharp chisel, cutting a mitre angle. Cut identical mitres on the end piece, slightly oversized, and trim back carefully to the line, taking very fine shavings until a good fit is achieved. Glue into place.

Cut all of the fret slots, being careful not to tear the purfling with the fret saw.

The assembly now requires the carving of a **radius**. See 'Carving a Radius Onto the Fingerboard' later in this section. Once the fingerboard with its purfling has had a radius carved, the edges of the fret slots will no longer be deep enough. This is easily rectified by re-cutting with a fret saw, being careful to follow the path of the original slot. If the saw is fitted with a depth stop, you can follow the camber of the fingerboard until the stop prevents the teeth from cutting any deeper.

Next run a triangular file over the tops of each slot to take off the sharp corners. Check once more that the slots are consistently deep and then glue the bindings onto the outside of the fingerboard in the same way as for the purflings. Allow to dry, and then trim the top of the bindings flush with the fingerboard's radius.

When the whole assembly is dry, remove the tape from underneath and plane the binding and purfling flush with the underside of the fingerboard blank.

Inlay lines being glued and sandwiched together between strips of perspex to make purfling.

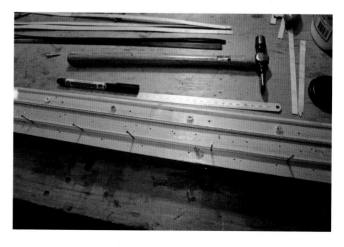

Purfling being glued on either side of the ebony fingerboard blank.

The point of a panel pin recessed into the workboard to hold the fingerboard blank.

The end purfling waiting to be glued onto the ebony fingerboard blank.

The end purfling being glued onto the ebony fingerboard blank.

The fret slots being cut with a saw with a depth stop.

The fingerboard radius being sanded onto the ebony blank.

Ebony binding being glued on in the same way as for the purfling.

Fret Position Markers and Side Dots

Unlike 'classical' guitars, most steel-string guitars have fret **position markers** on the front of the fingerboard and on the side of the fingerboard facing the player. Position markers can be anything from simple inlaid dots to complicated mother-of-pearl inlays – the choice is yours. For the sake of simplicity, the guitars featured here have 5mm (³⁄₁₆in) mother-of-pearl dots inlaid on the face and small 2mm (⁵⁄₆₄in) mother-of-pearl dots on the side.

Traditionally the fret markers are positioned at the third, fifth, seventh, ninth, twelfth (×2), fifteenth and seventeenth frets, and sometimes the nineteenth fret. The **side dots** can follow the same pattern, but invariably it is deemed only necessary to go up to the twelfth (octave) fret position.

POSITION MARKERS

To ascertain the centre of a dot position marker, draw two diagonals across the fret space from each fret position. The place where they cross will be the centre of the marker. Mark this point with a bradawl to centre the drill bit.

A spur drill bit is best for excavating the hole for the inlay, as it will give a flat-bottomed hole and allow the mother of pearl to sit in a level and even position. Drill just deep enough so that the inlay sits almost flush with the fingerboard's surface. Any excess protrusion can be scraped level once it is glued in. Drop a globule of epoxy glue into the hole, push the dot into it, hold it down with tape and allow the glue to dry thoroughly.

Holes for side dots being drilled into the edge of the fingerboard blank.

Side dots being glued into the edge of a fingerboard.

SIDE DOTS

Clamp the fingerboard onto a piece of square timber, with the edge of the fingerboard that needs drilling horizontal with the drill press table. Clamp a straight back stop behind to the table so that the fingerboard assembly can be slid along it so all of the holes will be in line.

Drill holes just deep enough so that the inlay sits almost flush with the fingerboard's surface in the positions required, drop a globule of epoxy glue into the hole, push the dot into it and hold down with tape and allow the glue to dry thoroughly. All inlays can then be smoothed flush by filing or sanding.

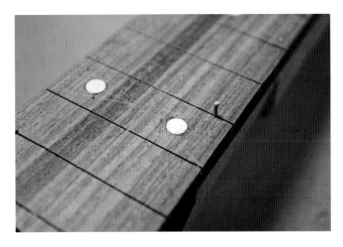

The fingerboard held in place with a panel pin through a hole in the fret slot.

The Fingerboard Extension Wedge

As the neck does not join the body on a horizontal plane, the fingerboard extension (the part of the fingerboard that lies from the neck/body joint to the soundhole) will not sit flat naturally onto the soundboard but will rise up by between 1mm and 2mm. To fill this gap a wedge needs to be fashioned that will fit precisely under the fingerboard extension. To ensure that the wedge is not intrusive it is usually made out of the same material as either the fingerboard, the neck or the soundboard.

Lay the fingerboard onto the neck and measure the maximum gap at the soundhole end. Prepare a piece of timber slightly thicker than this measurement and 3mm (⅛in) wider and longer than the fingerboard extension.

When the fingerboard is eventually fixed on, it needs to be glued exactly in the right position on the neck and across the soundboard to the soundhole. It must not be allowed to slip out of position whilst being glued, so it has to be locked into position to avoid this. Small panel pins are ideal for this, so tight-fitting holes need to be drilled into the fingerboard to accommodate them.

Drill a small hole, the same diameter as a small panel pin (no bigger than 1.5mm) through the first fret slot. It is important that the pin fits the hole precisely with no movement, so do a practice hole on a piece of scrap hardwood to determine a good fit. Drill to one side of the fingerboard, as the centre will be directly above the truss rod. Drill a second hole diagonally opposite the first in the eleventh fret slot. Drill further pin holes through the thirteenth fret and the twentieth fret, again diagonally opposite each other. (These pin holes will all be covered up by the fret wire once it is installed.)

Place the fingerboard onto the neck, ensuring that the

The fingerboard extension and wedge blank held in place with panel pins.

The fingerboard extension wedge blank held in place with panel pins.

centre lines correspond and that the narrow end of the fingerboard is sitting at the position that will be the front of the nut (commonly 5mm or ³⁄₁₆in from the headstock angle) and clamp into place temporarily. Push a panel pin into each of the first and eleventh fret holes and then tap them lightly to enable an impression to be made in the neck's surface.

The fingerboard extension wedge blank being glued on and clamped with a wooden clamping caul.

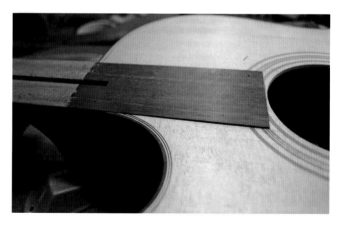

The fingerboard extension wedge flattened and levelled with the neck.

Unclamp and remove the fingerboard, and with the same drill bit bore the pin impressions 3mm (⅛in) to 4mm (⁵⁄₃₂in) deep.

Relocate the fingerboard and insert two pins to lock it into place. Lift off the neck slightly and slide the wedge material under the extension, ensuring that it pushes right up to the neck joint position and has an equal overlap around its perimeter. Drill again with the same bit through the pin holes in frets thirteen and twenty and through the wedge material and the soundboard. Push panel pins through these new holes to lock the wedge material into place.

Score with a sharp knife around the fingerboard extension onto the wedge material to reproduce its outline. Remove the pins and the fingerboard, and trim the wedge exactly to the scored line. Now glue the wedge material into place, using the two pins to locate and lock it into position. Clamp this assembly in place using a couple of clamps through the soundhole with a clamping caul that has pin clearance holes and allow the glue to dry.

Finally, remove the two pins and plane down the wedge so that it forms a level surface with the neck. Check for flatness regularly with a long straight edge. Note that the leading edge of the wedge next to the neck joint will be planed to practically nothing.

Gluing on the Fingerboard

Before gluing, check the alignment of the fingerboard one more time by locating it with all four pins and ensuring that there is no movement. Also check that the underside of the fingerboard is flat, especially across its width. Any unevenness or lumps present will prevent the edges of the board from gluing down flat. To ensure that this is achieved, it is perfectly acceptable to very slightly hollow the underside with a scraper (the emphasis being on very slightly!). This way, when glued down the fingerboard edges will be free of gaps.

To spread the clamping pressure, make a wooden caul that

The cauls and clamps for gluing on the fingerboard sitting ready following a dry run.

The fingerboard glued on and clamped with a wooden caul.

Masking tape applied to the truss rod slot to prevent glue from fouling the rod.

is the same length and width as the fingerboard, complete with four clearance holes that will allow it to slot over the locating pins.

It is important that no glue gets into the truss rod slot, and consequently the moving parts of the truss rod itself, so stick 25mm (1in) wide masking tape over and along the complete length of the truss rod slot.

PROTECTING THE TRUSS ROD SLOT

Laying masking tape over and along the truss rod slot will ensure this area remains glue-free. When the fingerboard is clamped down, any excess glue will spread into the tape area but not into the slot.

Apply glue to the surface of the neck and to the face of the wedge (not to the fingerboard), pull off the tape, locate and pin the fingerboard, place the caul over and clamp it down. Use further wooden cauls under the neck to avoid damage from the clamps. Use approximately six to eight G-clamps along the neck and two clamps through the soundhole to hold down the fingerboard extension. Allow the glue to dry thoroughly.

Despite every attempt to plane all components level and even, it is not unusual to find that following the clamping and gluing process the fingerboard is no longer entirely flat. Take this opportunity to check and level it if necessary.

Carving a Radius Onto the Fingerboard

Unlike 'classical guitar' fingerboards, which are invariably flat across their widths, fingerboards on steel-string guitars commonly have a radius carved onto them.

It is best to plane the majority of the radius first and then finish with a proprietary sanding block. As you work, check that the radius is consistent and doesn't round off at the edges of the fingerboard.

Carving a radius will inevitably lead to the ends of the fret slots becoming too shallow, so they need re-cutting to the required depth. Set the depth stop on the fret saw and then deepen the slots, following the arch of the radius until a consistent depth is achieved. Some manufacturers get around this by initially cutting their fret slots over-deep so that once a radius has been applied the ends of the slots are not too shallow. However, this can have a detrimental effect on the strength the fingerboard adds to the neck.

The fingerboard radius being checked with a gauge.

The fingerboard being radiussed: note the use of a mask to avoid any slips marking the soundboard.

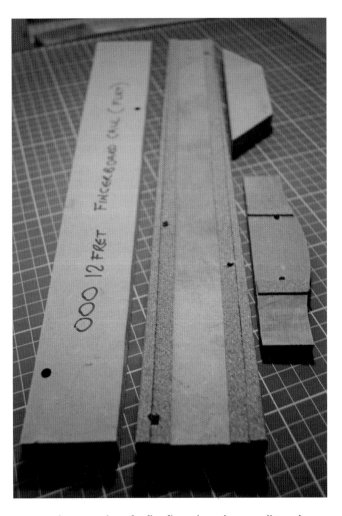

Cauls: examples of a flat fingerboard, pre-radiussed fingerboard, bridge plate and bridge gluing caul.

Trimming the neck stem flush with the fingerboard.

GLUING ON A FINGERBOARD WITH A PRE-CARVED RADIUS

If, as in the case of a bound version, the fingerboard has a radius before being glued to the neck then a special clamping caul has to be used to ensure that it glues flat to the neck surface.

Once the fingerboard is glued on and profiled, take this opportunity to trim any excess width from the neck so that it is flush with the fingerboard.

A clamp-on vice used to hold neck when working on it.

Installing the Frets

CHOOSING THE CORRECT FRET SIZE AND TYPE

Fret size is often a matter of taste, but if you are not sure what type to fit do try out different 'off-the-peg' guitars. Take note of the frets that are installed on the instrument that suits you best. Acoustic guitar frets do not tend to vary as greatly as those on electric guitars, but in general the following information may help your choice.

Height   A tall fret wire (anything over 1.15mm or 0.045in) is often preferred by string benders and this can produce a good, clear note without a lot of finger pressure. However, if you are prone to pressing the strings down hard, the height of the fret can make the string play sharp. Low fret wire can feel a bit insignificant, although it is preferred by some. If you are not a string bender, then this type may suit your playing style.

Width   Wide fret wire (anything over 2.5mm or 0.110in) is more commonly found on electric guitars. Unless they are consistently domed, however, they offer too flat a surface, which can have intonation implications. Narrow or skinny fret wire (that below 2.0mm or 0.080in) is more commonly used on banjos and mandolins, or on vintage instruments like nineteenth-century guitars.

Material   The most common fret wire material is often quoted as being nickel, but this can vary in quality somewhat, with often the cheaper brands being inferior by being too soft and consequently not hard wearing. A superior version is one that is cited as being 18 per cent nickel–silver.

You can obtain fret wire that is made of stainless steel, which is very hard wearing, but this is very tricky to install. As it also has very little flexibility the wire has to be bent to precisely the same camber as the fingerboard, otherwise it will not seat down consistently along its length. There is also a version available known as EVO Copper Alloy. This has the advantage of being nickel-free.

The fret wire used on the guitars here is Dunlop 6190, which has a width of 2.13mm (0.084in), a crown height of 1.0mm (0.039in) and a tang of 1.4mm (0.055in).

CUTTING AND PREPARING THE FRETS

When all of the fret slots are cut, and the depth of each has been checked, run a small triangular needle file across the top of each slot to take off the sharp corners. This will help to reduce the likelihood of wood breakout if a fret has to be removed because you are dissatisfied with its installation or during a future **re-fret**. This will also help with initial positioning of the fret tang during insertion.

Each piece of fret wire should have a slightly tighter curve than the profile or camber of the fingerboard. This is most conveniently achieved by running a sufficient length of fret wire through a fret bender. These devices have adjustable rollers through which the wire passes to bend it to the correct curvature. The frets are then cut individually from this length. If a fret bender is not available, cut the frets and then curve each one carefully utilizing a padded pair of pliers at each end.

To avoid wastage, cut frets in sets of three. Measure the longest of the three, add 3mm (⅛in) at each end and cut all three frets that length. Then cut the next three, all the same length as the longest of that set. If the fingerboard is bound, as in Guitar #1, the frets need to be cut to the exact length of each fret position (*see* 'Fretting Bound Fingerboards' later in this section).

A wooden fret holder is invaluable for keeping frets in the correct order; this consists of a wooden base with numbered holes. The holder pictured here has three sets of holes, which is essential for guitar re-frets – one set for the old removed frets, the second set for the new replacements and the third for spares.

HAMMERING IN FRETS

It is strongly recommended that the technique of hammering in frets is practised on a test piece first. This is a skill like any other, which gets better with experience.

The idea is to hammer home the fret in as few hits as possible (three to four is a good goal), which will reduce the risk of distorting the fret wire. The guitar's neck must be steady and fully supported, thereby reducing the possibility of bounce or recoil, which in turn will lessen the effectiveness of each hit of the hammer. In other words, make each strike count!

Ensure the instrument is on a firm, padded surface. Devise

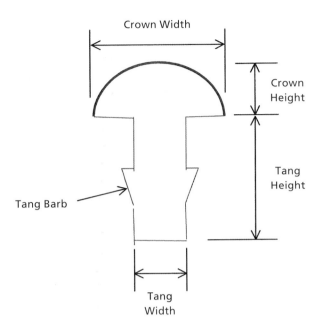

Diagram of the fret wire profile.

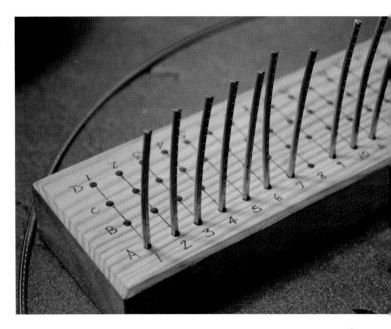

Frets located in a numbered block awaiting installation.

a way of holding the guitar body steady so that there is no movement. The back of the neck immediately behind the slot to be fretted must have a very solid block in place so the neck is fully supported whilst inserting the fret. If the rear of the neck is already carved, then an appropriately shaped and adequately padded neck support must be used. If you have opted to carve the neck after the frets have been installed, a substantial block of wood can be utilized. Some makers use a heavy-duty bag filled with shot, which moulds itself to the neck's contour and affords good support to the neck. Whatever is used, there must be no possibility of any bounce or movement.

When hammering in the frets, an appropriate tool must be used. The hammer used here is known as a 'dead blow'. The hammer's head is half-filled with shot, which falls to the face of the head, thus reducing bounce.

Some hit the end of the fret wire and work along its length until it is fully installed. Others hammer the centre of the fret wire first and then work out to each end. The argument for doing it this way is that the barbs on the fret tang dig into the fingerboard sideways and hold the fret more

A fret bender applying the correct radius onto the fret wire.

Rubber door wedges make good supports for guitar bodies.

Hammering in the frets.

firmly. Whichever method you choose, you want to avoid the ends coming up when the centre is struck. Experiment with different ways until you find a technique with which you are happy.

Smear a bead of aliphatic glue along the bottom of the

fret's tang. This will not only help to lubricate and ease installation, but it will also help to hold the frets in place (*see* 'Removing Frets' later in this section).

Place the fret with an equal overhang either side of the fingerboard and ensure that the fret is standing perfectly

Clipping flush the fret ends.

A heavy lump of lead to be placed under the fingerboard extension when hammering in frets.

Pulling fret wire through a 'fret barber' to reduce the size of tang barbs.

upright. Hammer in the fret, checking that it is seated fully along its length, and wipe away any glue squeeze-out with a damp cloth. Once all the frets are installed in this way leave the assembly for the relevant time to allow the glue to harden.

Trim the fret ends flush with the fingerboard using a pair of fret cutters. Use the cutters sideways, as the leverage of

using them upright can cause the fret end to rise up out of the slot.

FRETTING THE FINGERBOARD EXTENSION

Fretting up to the neck/body joint is fairly straightforward as long as the precautions previously stated are adhered to.

Hammering in frets in the fingerboard extension. Note the need to hold the solid block inside through the soundhole.

Once you start fretting the fingerboard extension you are hammering over the soundboard, and as you are now over an area that is hopefully a beautifully resonant **soundbox**, the noise can be quite terrifying. Also, without adequate support there is a very real danger that the soundboard could distort or crack. Placing a substantial block (such as a lump of lead) inside and under the fingerboard extension will absorb a lot of the shock from hammering.

One way of helping with fret installation in this area is to remove some of the width of the tang's barbs. This can be achieved by pulling the fret wire through a 'fret barber', which files a small amount off the barbs, thus easing the fret's insertion into the slot. This technique is also sometimes necessary when hammering frets into very hard woods like ebony.

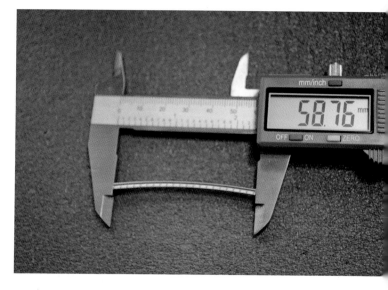

Measuring a fret to a precise length for installation in a bound fingerboard.

PRESSING IN FRETS

Some makers press in rather than hammer in frets. This is normally done with the aid of an arbor press, fitted with specialist fret press cauls that are shaped to the fingerboard radius. This can save some time in a workshop that regularly makes and repairs guitars, but it is questionable if the expense is worth it for the occasional maker. It has also to be pointed out that you can only use this method on an acoustic guitar on frets up to the neck heel/body joint. There are alternative presses for installing frets above this

The fret wire ends being carefully ground to length.

Frets awaiting installation on the bound fingerboard.

A fret tang end cut back prior to installation in a bound fingerboard.

This does mean that installing the frets is more complicated and time consuming, but the end result is often deemed worthwhile.

After curving a sufficient length of fret wire on the fret bender, each fret has to be cut exactly to length. Because the fret slot is stopped short by the binding, the tang at each end of the fret has to be cut back by the same amount. This can be done with a small needle file or, better still, with a specialist 'fret tang nipper'.

Install the frets in the same manner as described above, but this time making sure that the fret is centralized across the width of the fingerboard. Also make especially sure that the ends are hammered down fully. (Note that because these frets are already to cut to length there is no need to trim so the next stage is bevelling.)

REMOVING FRETS

If you have to remove a fret for any reason, this must be done carefully to avoid damaging the fingerboard, especially the edges of the fret slots. A pair of nippers ground flat across the top of the cutting edges is ideal, or a specialist fret puller (essentially the same thing) can be used. It is worthwhile warming the fret first to soften any glue that may have been used, usually with a soldering iron. Open the jaws of the nipper either side of the fret and gently close them onto the

point, but again they are only really suitable for the regular builder.

FRETTING BOUND FINGERBOARDS

Apart from aesthetics, the main reason for binding a finger-board is that the fret ends are concealed behind the edging.

Checking the depth of the fret slot: if the mark on the strip appears above the fret slot, it is not deep enough.

Fret slots on a bound fingerboard being deepened and cleaned out with specialist saw.

fret wire, coaxing up the fret as you close the jaws together. Do not yank upwards as this could cause the fret tang bards to pull up excessive shards of wood. Instead, walk the nipper across the fret, gently opening and closing the jaws as you go, allowing the natural lifting action of the closing jaws to persuade the fret to rise up. Repeat several times until the fret wire comes up and away naturally.

Ensure you clean any old glue from the slot and check that it is sufficiently and consistently deep before installing a new fret.

Filing a bevel onto the fret ends.

Manicuring the fret ends to remove any sharp corners.

TRIMMING AND BEVELLING FRET ENDS

On unbound fingerboards, run a flat file held vertically along the side of the fingerboard to smooth flush all fret ends. Mask off the soundboard either side of the fingerboard extension to avoid accidental marring of the surface. Be careful not to take off any wood, so stop when the file stops grinding metal.

The fret ends now require bevelling. The same engineer's flat file can be run along the fret ends, this time angled at approximately 35 degrees to the edge of the fingerboard. To maintain a consistent angle, it is well worth making up a file block as illustrated.

Try not to scrub backwards and forwards but instead run the file from one end of the fingerboard to the other to obtain a consistent line of bevelled ends. Repeat until the file has just started to take off the sharp corner of the wooden fingerboard.

This operation will have angled all of the fret ends, but will have left each bevel with two very sharp corners. These need rounding off with a fine file, as if you were manicuring your nails. A file with a smooth safety edge is best, as this will prevent marring the fingerboard. Specialist fret end dressing files are available from luthier suppliers for this purpose.

LEVELLING THE FRETS

With the best will in the world, it is almost impossible to install all frets in an identical fashion, so the chances are that they will not be entirely level with each other. The frets all being even and on the same plane is vital for buzz-free playing, however, so this stage has to be carried out carefully and methodically. The following description is relevant not only to newly installed frets but also to frets on older instruments where play and wear has necessitated a fret re-dress.

First, ensure that the neck is straight by sighting down it from the nut end; any curve should hopefully be fairly obvious. If you do not trust your eyesight, however, then a straight edge should be utilized. The problem is that you will have to lay the straight edge on top of the frets, which without being levelled will give a false reading. Specialist straight edges are available from luthier suppliers, which overcome this problem by bridging each fret as they are notched in the relevant places. They therefore read the fingerboard, not the frets. (Be aware, however, that these specialist notched straight edges are expensive and you will need different ones for alternative scale lengths.)

To avoid scarring the fingerboard's surface whilst fret levelling, the fingerboard needs to be masked off with tape.

CUSTOMIZE YOUR MASKING TAPE

Due to the fact that fret redressing and re-frets are a regular repair job, reels of wide 50mm (2in) low-tack tape can be bought and cut to convenient widths on the bandsaw, namely 25mm (1in), 12.7mm (½in) and 8mm (⁵⁄₁₆in). These widths tend to be suitable for masking off all of the fingerboard surfaces between the frets, even up to the highest that are very close together.

Masking the fingerboard to avoid damage from the fret leveller.

The fret leveller: a diamond stone held in a wooden handle by strong magnets.

A very flat file or stone is required to level the frets. The tool used here is a medium diamond stone held in a workshop-built wooden holder with magnets.

The stone is run from one end of the fingerboard to the other, being careful to follow any fingerboard radius. This will flatten the top of the highest frets but miss any that are lower. It is therefore necessary to repeat the stoning until all of the frets have been touched. Once this happens, in theory, you should have fret tops that are all level with each other. Check with a conventional straight edge to confirm that this is the case.

TAKE CARE

If it becomes obvious that any one fret is being reduced in height dramatically before the adjacent frets have even been touched, it may be worth replacing that fret, as the chances are it was not seated properly when hammered in.

All of the frets will now have a flat surface or scored marks where the levelling stone has passed over. As in any filing or sanding operation, going up through finer grades of abrasive will slowly but surely eliminate deeper marks from the previous abrasive. The next tool to achieve this is an offcut from an old spirit level that has a different grade of wet-and-dry abrasive stuck to each flat face, in this case 240 and 400. This is passed over all of the frets from one end of the

The fret leveller being run along the tops of the frets.

Re-profiling the frets after the leveller has flattened their crowns.

A fret rocker being used to check the frets are level with each other.

fingerboard to the other, first with the coarse side, then with the finer.

The fret tops now have to be re-profiled to restore their curved cross-section. This can be done by running a small file along each fret and shaping the dome back into shape, but the best tool for this is a specialist fret file, which has a concave file edge. First run an indelible pen across the top of each fret, and then run the fret crowning file along the length of each fret, carefully re-profiling whilst being careful not to eliminate the pen mark fully. This will help to ensure that the peaks of the fret tops are still level with each other.

You should now have a set of frets that are all level with each other, with their cross-sectional shape having been re-profiled to a consistent curve, which ensures that the string is only touching the peak of the fret when held down onto the fingerboard. Check once more that the frets are all level by laying a straight edge across the tops of all of them and, with a good light source behind, check for any gaps at all. It could be that you have one errant fret that prevents the straight edge from lying evenly across all of the frets, in which case this can be identified by checking groups of frets to see which one is higher than its neighbours.

DRESSING THE FRETS

Following the preceding processes the fret wire will not be smooth enough, as it will still bear the scars from filing and so on. These need to be eliminated to result in smooth, highly polished frets that will stop strings cleanly without any catching or scratchiness.

The next stage, therefore, is to sand each fret wire progressively until there are no obvious marks or scratches in evidence, for which detail sanding pens are used. In the guitars shown here three different grades have been used – 180 grit, 320 grit and 400 grit. Each pen has been modified on the end of the angled face by having a semi-circular groove filed into it with a round needle file. This enables the sanding belt to form to the curve of the fret profile. Carefully sand along each fret, smoothing out any deep scratches, repeat with a finer grade, and then finish with the finest. This will hopefully have resulted in smooth, scratch-free frets.

To go the extra mile, all frets should then be polished with a proprietary metal polish and buffed to a shine with a clean cotton cloth, or with a polishing mother-of-pearl attachment on the Dremel mini tool. This process is very time-consuming, but worth all the effort.

The Bridge

Bridges come in various shapes, from plain to very elaborate and stylistic. One important thing to remember is that the bridge should be considered as an additional brace to the soundboard. The larger it is, therefore, the more it will resist the movement of the top and consequently dampen its vibrations and resonance. It does, however, have to be substantial enough to withstand the considerable pull from the strings. As it is glued directly to the soundboard and is not normally mechanically affixed, it requires a sufficient gluing area to keep it in place. A commonly agreed ideal size for glued bridges is 150mm (6in) long by 25mm (1in) wide.

The main centre section houses the saddle and the bridge pins (if these are used). The top of this section should be curved to match the camber of the fingerboard. The wings of the bridge can be dressed away somewhat to lighten the structure, whilst still maintaining the maximum gluing surface. It is also worth considering rounding off edges and corners on which the player may rest their hand.

To ensure that the bridge fits perfectly, the first job is to carve the underside of the bridge blank to match the dome of the soundboard. This is best achieved whilst the blank is oversized, as if attempted when the bridge is at its final dimensions it is all too easy to carve off an excessive amount, which can reducing the height to below the required measurement.

A jig to create the initial curve is illustrated opposite; a screw is adjusted under the sanding plate to increase or decrease its arch. The soundboard dome can be measured with a profile gauge and then the jig set up to mimic this curve.

Sand in long, even strokes, checking regularly that the underside of the bridge blank is obtaining a consistent arch along its length whilst remaining flat across its width. This method will get the bridge blank close to fitting. However, a bit of fine tuning by using a small scraper to remove any irregularities and smooth the sanded surface will usually be required.

It is important that the blank can be placed in position on the soundboard and that there are no gaps. Press down on one end and check that it doesn't lift at the other. Repeat this with diagonal corners. If any rocking movement is observed, then more contouring is required. Only when you are satisfied that the blank fits as well as it can should you proceed with the bridge shaping.

The bridge detailed here is a version of the pyramid bridge made famous by Martin guitars. As the inner face of the

The bridge blank having an initial arch sanded onto the bottom face.

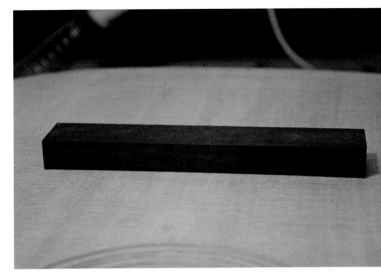

The bridge blank being fitted to the soundboard dome.

pyramid curves back up to the centre section, it helps to drill holes to create the transition. Two faces are then cut on the bandsaw and smoothed. The third and fourth faces are then fashioned, first with a coarse file and then by smoothing with scrapers or sanding blocks.

Next, mark out and centre-punch the bridge pin centres. Initially drill pilot holes in each position, the size of which should match a panel pin.

The bridge blank should then be secured to a square of scrap wood by inserting panel pins through the outer bridge

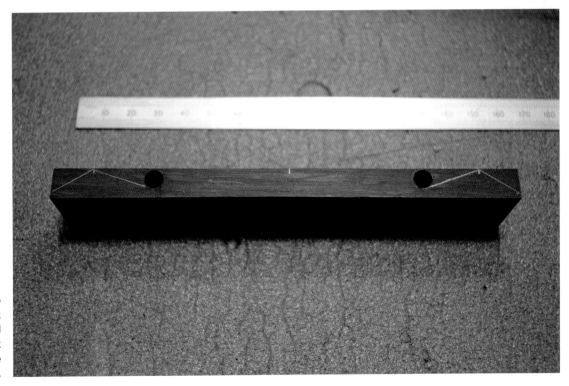

Holes drilled in into the bridge blank where the pyramid ends curve back up to the centre section.

139

The pyramid section on the bridge blank cut out using a bandsaw.

The pyramid faces being filed on: note the bridge blank is pinned onto a wooden jig held in a vice.

pin pilot holes. This enables the safe cutting of the top arch. Ensure that the heads of the panel pins are countersunk sufficiently to be below the line of the cut. The whole bridge should then be smoothed using consecutively finer abrasives.

It is possible to rout the saddle slot at this stage, in which case a jig has to be made to allow the router to cut an angled slot in the correct place. However, many makers prefer to position the saddle exactly once the bridge is glued on to the soundboard (*see* Chapter 7 for details).

Intonation

This next piece of information may come as a bit of a shock. Although we consider modern scales and tunings to be 'equal tempered', many musical instruments, including guitars, invariably play slightly 'out of tune' and the fretting, action and set-up is therefore normally a bit of a compromise. While you absorb this alarming and treasonous news, here is an explanation that will hopefully put your mind at rest.

The calculated fret positions are based on a string length which is, in fact, a 'nominal' string length. In reality, this has to be altered slightly to compensate for variances in string tension, string diameter, fret size and so on.

When you stretch a string between two points (in this instance the saddle and the nut) this is known as the instrument's string length, and its halfway point is an octave (twelve semitones) up from the open played note. Therefore the twelfth fret is positioned directly under this point. This is all very well and good until you want to fret this note and pull the string down onto the fingerboard just behind the twelfth fret.

When the string is pressed down you can observe that the point of contact on top of the twelfth fret is no longer the string's halfway mark. There is now more string between the twelfth fret, passing under your finger and to the nut, than there is from the twelfth fret to the saddle. This is a slightly simplistic way of looking at it, as this also involves altering the tension of the string, but it illustrates the problem fairly clearly. One way around this is to lengthen the distance from the twelfth fret to the saddle to make it the same as the fretted string length from the twelfth fret to the nut. Consequently, the saddle position must be sited

The bridge blank pinned to wooden block to cut the top curve safely.

The bridge blank with a rough-cut top curve.

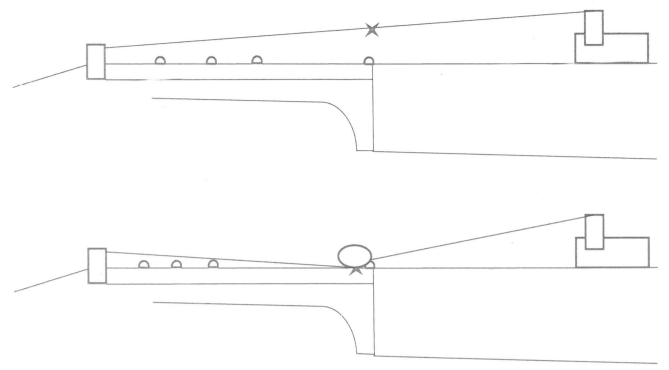

A diagram showing variances in string height and intonation when a string is pressed.

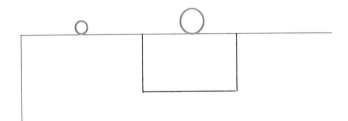

Saddle ramped back to adjust string point of contact.

further back from its 'nominal' position to compensate for this irregularity.

You may have noticed that on a steel-string guitar the saddle is angled across the bridge, making the bass strings slightly longer than the treble strings. This is necessary as the diameter of the strings on a steel-string vary quite dramatically from treble to bass, as does their tension, so the fatter-wound bass string requires a longer 'speaking' length than the thin treble.

You may have also noted that nylon-strung 'classical' guitars usually have a saddle that runs straight across the bridge. The reason for this is that there is very little

difference in string diameter from treble to bass, so even though the saddle is set back for intonation purposes, the strings work well enough if they all share the same 'speaking' length.

Again, this is a bit of a generalization, but the treble side of the steel-string saddle is commonly set back about 2mm (⁵⁄₆₄in) from the 'nominal' string length, and the bass side of the saddle is set back approximately 4mm (⁵⁄₃₂in) from the 'nominal' string length.

For example, for an instrument that is built to have a 650mm (25.59in) string length, the actual string length on the treble side, from nut to saddle, will be 652mm (25.67in), whilst the bass side, from nut to saddle, will be 654mm (25.75in). This arrangement is still a bit of a compromise, however, as each string's correct point of contact depends on its gauge, tension and type (plain or wound).

This is well demonstrated by looking at the bridge of an electric guitar, which has six individual bridge pieces, to see how they are positioned to obtain accurate intonation. You will notice opposite that, although the first and sixth saddle pieces are angled back across the bridge, the positions of the other saddles do not fall into a straight line between the two. Strings one, two and three are in a reasonably straight line

The bridge on an electric guitar showing the layout for correct intonation when using a plain third string.

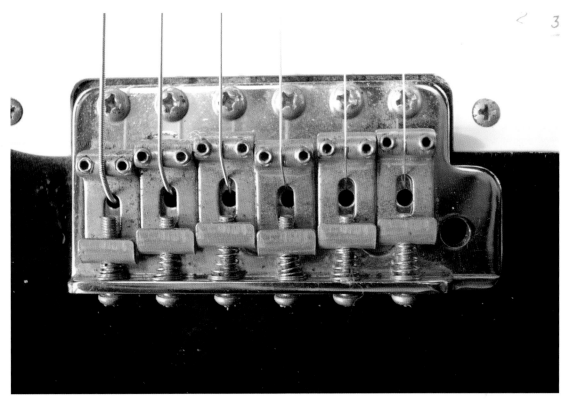

The bridge on an electric guitar showing the layout for correct intonation when using a wound third string.

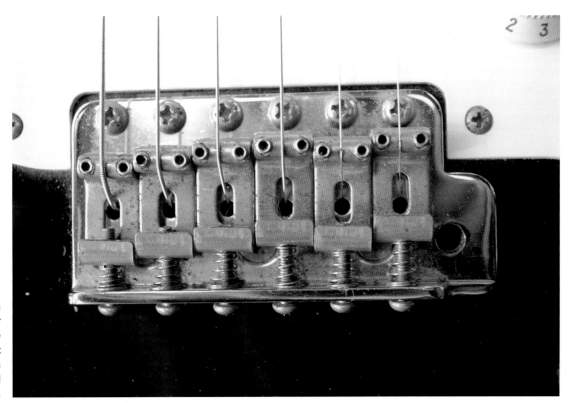

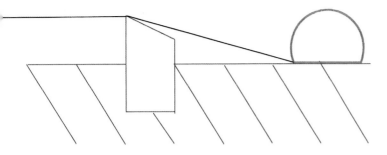

The string point of contact at the front of the saddle.

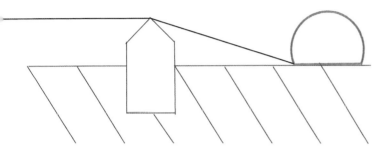

The string point of contact at the middle of the saddle.

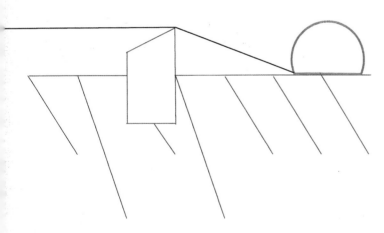

The string point of contact at the back of the saddle.

with each other, as are strings four, five and six, but the third is set back further than the fourth.

This arrangement is a common set-up for a set of strings that has a plain third string. If, as is more common on a steel-string guitar, a wound third string is used, then the layout is more likely to be that in the second illustration.

It is possible to replicate this arrangement on a fixed (non-adjustable) saddle by altering the string's point of contact. This is done by shaping the saddle where the individual string passes across its thickness, as below. As saddles are commonly approximately 3mm (⅛in) thick, you can alter the point of contact across the saddle. Some makers, like Ervin Samogyi, advocate the use of a thicker saddle nearer to 5mm (³⁄₁₆in), which allows even greater adjustment for each string (*see* Chapter 7 for how this is achieved in practice).

Gluing on the Bridge

The soundboard must be fully smoothed and finished before gluing on the bridge. If the guitar has had a spray finish and the bridge area has been masked off, then remove the tape and ensure that the gluing area consists of clean, smooth and bare wood.

It cannot be stressed enough that this is probably one of the most important joints to get right. As the integrity of the bridge relies on the glued joint, the fit between the bridge and the soundboard must correspond exactly.

Check one last time that the bridge can be placed onto the soundboard with no gaps discernable whatsoever. Press down on one corner and observe the corner diagonally opposite. There must be no movement. Repeat with the other corners. Only proceed when satisfied that the fit is good.

Make up a wooden caul that is at least the same length and width as the bridge, padding it with strips of cork to allow it to fit on top of the bridge's curve. For a pyramid-type bridge, a square of cork can be glued onto the underside of the caul above the pyramid's point.

Mount the bridge in the correct position. This can be ascertained by measuring the correct string length falling into the centre of the saddle position (*see* the previous section) and that it is centralized with relation to the neck and string path. One way is to hold a straight edge on the string path of the first and last strings, lining up the outside bridge pins and ensuring that the gap down the edge of the neck is the same for both strings.

Push a panel pin through the outside bridge pin pilot holes to make an impression in the soundboard. Remove the bridge and drill with the pilot drill right through the soundboard and bridge plate. Replace the bridge and lock it into place with two pins. Check one last time that the bridge is in the correct position and at 90 degrees to the centre line. If by chance this

Cumpiano does this much better

On an acoustic twelve-string guitar, each pair of strings passes over the saddle at the same point of contact as each other. For the paired strings that contain a fat wound string and a thin plain string (tuned an octave apart) this, as previously discussed, is somewhat of an anomaly. The larger diameter wound string needs a different point of contact than the thin plain string for intonation purposes – so how can this work? Well, in theory, it doesn't! However, this is probably what gives twelve-string guitars their characteristic sound – slightly dissonant. Having heard a twelve-string with individual saddle pieces each adjusted for correct intonation, they do sound different, even slightly bland, so this could be an example of our ears getting used to and accepting a certain sound.

is no longer the case, remove the offending pin, square up the bridge and replace the pin in the adjacent hole.

Mount two bridge clamps through the soundhole, place the wooden caul on top of the bridge and clamp it in place. Ensure that the clamps have cleared any bracing and that they are bearing on the bridge plate. It is sometimes necessary to tape a small padded block to the bottom jaw of the clamp to ensure that this is so. If the bridge has trimmed down wings then fashion wedges that can be slid under the caul to make sure the wings are held firmly to the soundboard.

Remove the clamps and caul, apply glue to the bottom of the bridge and re-clamp the assembly. If the bridge has been fitted to the soundboard properly then it will not be necessary to tighten the clamps excessively. A good sign that the bridge is a good fit is a small line of glue squeeze-out around the perimeter. Do not be tempted to wipe this away, as not only is there a danger that you could disturb the clamps, but what you probably will do is smear glue into the soundboard grain. This will dry and resist any finish, making the overall effect a bit blotchy. Rather wait until it is dry and then carefully cut it away with a very sharp chisel.

The pyramid bridge being glued on: note the purpose-made caul holding down the pyramid wings.

The bridge being glued on with specialist clamps: note the caul and wedges holding down the bridge wings.

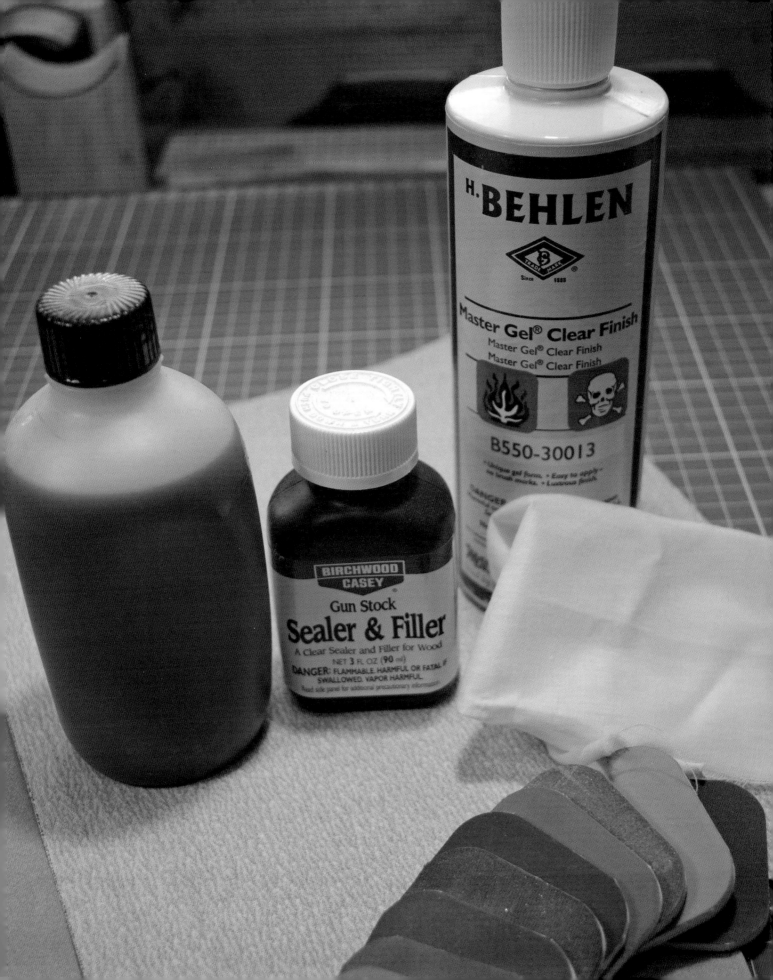

H. BEHLEN

Master Gel® Clear Finish

Master Gel® Clear Finish
Master Gel® Clear Finish

B550-30013

BIRCHWOOD
CASEY

Gun Stock
Sealer & Filler

A Clear Sealer and Filler for Wood
NET 3 FL OZ (90 ml)

DANGER: FLAMMABLE. HARMFUL OR FATAL IF
SWALLOWED. VAPOR HARMFUL

CHAPTER SIX

FINISHING

Applying a Finish

Before deciding what finish you are going to apply to your instrument, it is worth determining certain factors beforehand.

Durability   Is the instrument going to be subjected to rough handling, long hot and sweaty pub gigs, and generally a tough working life? If so, a hard-wearing spray lacquer finish may be suitable.

On the other hand, is your guitar going to be mollycoddled, lovingly cared for and generally receive more care and attention than your spouse or the cat? In which case a hand-applied oil finish could be the answer.

Finish Appearance   Do you want to see your face in a hard, shiny and glass-like finish, or would you prefer it to be matt, sinking into the wood's surface and looking more organic?

Facilities   Do you have the space, equipment and indeed the skill and patience to apply your preferred finish? You can always get a specialist workshop to apply that lacquer spray, but won't you then feel slightly cheated that you haven't completed the project yourself?

There are several different finishes traditionally used on musical instruments.

Spray Finishes

These often involve using lacquers such as nitro-cellulose or acid catalyzed, which can give a very consistent, durable

Just some of the finishing supplies used on guitars.

and glossy finish. However, their application is fraught with problems for the amateur or small-scale maker. A dedicated area that is dust-free and well ventilated needs to be available to successfully apply these types of finishes. It also needs to be consistently warm to allow the lacquers to cure properly. There are also health and safety issues to consider such as the breathing in of noxious fumes, which will necessitate wearing a mask and breathing apparatus.

Hand Finishes

FRENCH POLISHING
This can give a superb finish, which tends to enhance the natural beauty of the woods by accentuating the figure and grain lines. It is not as durable as some lacquers, but it is relatively easy to repair if knocks and scrapes need to be put right. However, to apply this finish successfully takes some practise, especially on a structure like a guitar. There exist some very good instruction videos (*see* Suggested Further Reading) that may be of help if you decide upon this finish.

VARNISH
Instruments of the violin family are traditionally finished with varnish and it can be equally successful when applied to guitars. Varnish can be brushed on, although, like all techniques, this takes some practise to perfect (*see* 'Applying an Oil Varnish' later in this chapter).

WIPING VARNISH
This is an oil varnish that has been thinned sufficiently to be applied with a cloth. It usually consists of a 1:2 to 1:3 varnish-to-thinner mix.

OIL

Although possibly not as durable as some of the previous methods mentioned, oil is the easiest finish to apply. If used correctly, oil can add a very attractive lustre to the wood and can be cut back to give a matt or semi-matt appearance.

There are several oils that can be used, including Boiled Linseed (which dries quicker than raw), Pure Tung, Teak and Danish. However, the one used most by instrument makers is Tru-Oil®, an American product from Birchwood Casey, which is primarily sold by firearms suppliers for coating gunstocks. It is a polymerized linseed oil with further natural oils added to it. Unlike some other oils it does build up a finish, although it remains thin and flexible, thus minimizing the damping effect on the wood's vibrations (see 'Applying an Oil Finish' later in this chapter).

Preparation

'Preparation is everything' is a phrase you will hear often when the subject of finishing is being discussed. It may sound like a hackneyed saying, but it is a sentiment to be embraced wholeheartedly. It is perfectly true that the more time and effort one puts into cleaning up, smoothing out and perfecting an instrument's surface, the better the final result will be. No matter what type of finish is applied, it will accentuate and make very obvious any scratches, dents, glue residue and so on. Having spent what can be a considerable amount of time, patience and money on building this incredible instrument, it is well worth putting in the extra time to get this part right. A few hours of hard work can make the difference between an instrument that looks professional, expertly built with a large amount of care invested, versus a messy, blotchy and rushed job.

As previously discussed, all of the guitar's components should be assembled carefully to produce gap-free joints and a neat appearance. It has also been stated that it is bad practice to rely on the use of filler to pack out any gaps created by imperfect joinery. However, with the best will in the world, especially for builders who are relatively inexperienced, it is likely that there will be the odd gap or dink. These must all be scrupulously filled and levelled before any finish is applied.

Filler

Filler should only be considered for hairline cracks or gaps. Anything larger should have slithers of the same wood fashioned and glued in to form the closest fit possible. It may even be worth considering replacing a section to produce a better result.

Proprietary wood fillers can be used, but it is sometimes easier and more effective if a paste is made up of the same wood's sawdust and glue, to be applied with an artist's palette knife. Ensure enough is pushed into the recess there is a sufficient amount to sit proud of the surface. Allow it to dry thoroughly before scraping or filing smooth.

Scraping

It has also been previously discussed that sanding all surfaces can create the problem of the dust from dark woods being ground into the surface of light coloured woods. Where possible it is better to use a very sharp scraper to level and even out bindings, inlays and so on. A new Stanley knife blade makes a very good scraper, which will cut quite keenly as long as the blade is regularly turned around to scrape from the other side. If ultimately the surface can only be flattened and smoothed with abrasives, try to avoid the bindings and inlays as much as possible.

Sanding

This stage should only be started when all of the guitar's components have been evened out and any glue residue, dinks, lumps and bumps have been scraped level.

Sanding a surface is only really effective if you work up through several grades of abrasive to achieve a suitable finish. Using a fine paper when the wood is still relatively rough, uneven and blemished will be hard work with very little result. Coarser abrasive will help to level and even, but this will obviously leave the surface covered with scratches from the size of the abrasive's grit. Therefore, it is necessary to follow this with a finer grade to eliminate the heavy scratches. This in turn will result in a scratched surface, but to a lesser degree. Subsequent use of steadily finer grades of grit will eventually

A baroque guitar (built by the author) hung in a U.V. cabinet to cure the varnish.

result in a surface that appears smooth with no obvious sanding lines.

Use a non-clogging abrasive paper such as silicon carbide or aluminium oxide. Start with grade 150, followed by 180, 220, 240, 280 and 320. Don't be tempted to skip a grade, so that each change of abrasive easily eliminates the scratches of the former. Wipe down the whole instrument between grades with a **tack cloth** to remove all dust before recommencing.

This should result in a smooth, blemish-free surface, which could be sufficient for applying a finish. However, it is well worth going that extra mile by continuing with an abrasive called Micro-Mesh™. This is a cloth-backed abrasive that was developed by the aerospace industry to remove scratches and marks from aeroplane windscreens. It can be bought in convenient sets and ranges in grades from 1500 to 12000. Again, it works best if all grades are used in sequence through to the finest. Although this is very labour-intensive, the results are really worth the effort. Because Micro-Mesh cuts rather than

sands, the resultant finish is super-smooth as it burnishes and polishes the wood, virtually sealing the surface and thereby making the application of a finish very much easier and more effective.

GOOD PRACTICE ADVICE: SANDING WITH ABRASIVES

- Cut the abrasive into relatively small squares and wrap around blocks. An oblong eraser makes a good block and because it is pliable it will conform to the guitar's curves.
- Sand in long strokes rather than scrubbing back and forth.
- It is possible to use Micro-Mesh across the grain of soundboards without scratching – this can enhance the wood's medullary rays.

A METHOD FOR FINISHING EARLY GUITARS

The following describes a method used for several years as a finishing for Early Guitars.

A yellow stain is first applied to all maple and spruce surfaces as a ground. The solution contains the following:

- 10g of fustic extract;
- 200ml of hot water;
- 20cc of alcohol (approx.).

First of all, all surfaces to be stained should be wetted with warm water to raise the grain. The fustic solution should then be applied to the soundboard, the sides and back, the rear of the neck and the rear and sides of the peghead/ headstock. Leave to dry in a U.V. cabinet.

Apply two further coats to the maple surface, leaving it to dry between coats. The spruce has only one coat, however, as the resultant colour is usually sufficient. The maple should then be burnished with a worn piece of garnet paper; the spruce can be burnished with wood shavings that have been saved from planing the soundboard.

Make up a grain filler containing silex (or mica) suspended in a mixture of oil varnish, boiled linseed oil and pure turpentine in equal volumes. (Note that the Silex drops to the bottom of the mixture if left for a while, so it will be necessary to stir the solution each time before use.)

Applied this to all surfaces, quite hard, with the aid of a French Polisher's rubber. All excess must be wiped off immediately with soft absorbent paper (such as kitchen roll or toilet tissue) and left until hard before applying further coats. Leave the guitar to dry completely in the U.V. cabinet.

Next, seal the soundboard with very thin clear varnish (a mix of approximately 6:1 of turpentine to varnish). The maple should then be coated with oil varnish diluted with turpentine to the right consistency. Four coats are necessary, with at least two days between coats to allow sufficient drying time. When the final coat is completely dry, rub all over very gently with 1200 wet-and-dry abrasive paper that has been wetted.

Polish the surface with a solution of 2:1 mix of boiled linseed oil to white spirit with two or three teaspoons of silex added. Apply gently and slowly with balls of cotton wool. This should then be wiped over with a soft cloth that is kept only for this purpose.

The ebony fingerboard and ebony veneers on the face and rear of the peghead should receive a couple of coats of thin linseed oil and silex. When dry, this should be rubbed over gently with 1200 wet-and-dry paper wetted with thin linseed oil and silex.

(My thanks to lute maker Stephen Gottlieb for this varnish method).

Applying an Oil Varnish

On very light woods such as maple you may decide to darken the wood slightly before applying a finish. This can be helped by leaving the instrument hung up in a U.V. cabinet (containing ultra violet tubes) for a few days to darken slightly. You may also decide to stain the wood.

A NOTE ON STAINS

If you decide to stain a wood surface, always try it out on a sample piece first. Be aware that staining certain woods such as spruce can sometimes result in a very inconsistent and blotchy finish.

Applying Pine Resin Varnish

Pine resin varnish has been in use for lacquering stringed musical instruments since the Middle Ages and is still the preferred finish for violins and copies of baroque instruments. It was also commonly in use on guitars until around the middle of the nineteenth century, after which time it became more usual to find them lacquered with shellac applied by French polishing.

It has the advantage not only of providing a protective coat to the instrument but of being flexible enough not to inhibit its vibrations. It is also reversible, in that if the finish is chipped or scratched it is possible to touch up and melt in new varnish to the old surface. It can be used in clear formulation but it also accepts pigment readily.

Applying an Oil Finish

If you want a finish that is approaching a lacquer finish in looks, you will need to fill the wood's pores first by applying a suitable grain filler. A filler compatible with Tru-Oil is available from the same manufacturer, but this is not essential. If, however, you have followed the preparation technique previously described and have a polished wood surface, the oil can be applied directly to the bare wood surface. This results in a very attractive open-pored finish that looks very natural.

A METHOD FOR FINISHING WITH PINE RESIN VARNISH

Various recipes are available in published form and can be sourced from Boutaine.[1] In preparing the varnish, typically 1kg of colophony is reduced to between a tenth and a quarter of its original weight, by heating at 250 degrees Celsius. The result is then mixed with one and a half times its weight in cold-pressed linseed oil and cooked further until it becomes elastic, and is then allowed to cool thoroughly. The mixture can then be diluted with pure rectified turpentine. Care must be taken at this point, as the mixture is volatile. The whole process emits strong fumes, taking up to thirty hours of cooking. It is therefore advisable to prepare the varnish either in a specially designed fume cabinet or outdoors.

A paste made of the varnish mixed with fine pumice, or mica, is rubbed in to the surface of the instrument, acting as both ground and grain filler. After twenty-four hours the varnish itself can be applied, either by brush or pad printing with palm of the hand.[2] Three to five coats are sufficient, allowing a day's drying time between each. Pumice lubricated with linseed oil can be used to de-nib between coats, which may be progressively thinned with a little more linseed oil. The final coat should be then be left for a minimum of a week to dry.

(My thanks to PhD student Nick Pyall for writing out this recipe and method, and to violin maker Shem Mackey for supplying the original information.)

[1] Boutaine, Jean-Louis, Stephane Vaiedelich and Jean-Philippe Echard, *De La Peinture De Chevalet a\0300 L'instrument De Musique: Vernis, Liants Et Couleurs*, Actes Du Colloque Des 6 Et 7 Mars 2007 (Paris: Muse\0301e de la musique, 2008).
[2] See Magister® Varnish Products at http://www.classicalvarnish.com (accessed 7 August 2011).

A METHOD FOR APPLYING THE OIL

Cut two pieces of lint-free cotton cloth (a bed sheet or old but clean T-shirt will suffice). It is a good idea to wear cotton gloves to prevent the natural oils on your hands from marring the surface.

Begin by wiping oil over a small surface (for example, for the back, ribs and soundboard, a quarter of the area at a time) and wipe off any excess immediately with the second cloth. Move on to the next area and repeat. Work relatively quickly and methodically, so as to prevent one area from drying and causing blending in with the adjacent area to be difficult. For areas such as the neck heel, make sure all excess oil is wiped away from corners; if left, they will take a lot longer to dry.

If the guitar is held by the neck, the whole body can be coated. Then hold the body by placing one hand through the soundhole with your thumb on the fingerboard extension to allow access to the neck and headstock.

Fashion an 'S' hook out of strong wire (wire coat hangers are ideal for this) and hang up the guitar to dry for several hours. If all has been done as described, the dried oil surface will be smooth to the touch. If there is any minor roughness, however, then the surface should be *very lightly* 'smoothed' with 0000-grade steel wool or a Scotch-Brite™ Grey sanding pad.

Apply further coats of oil in the same manner as before, using clean cloths each time. Four coats commonly results in a good sheen on the wood's surface, but this can depend on the wood type. Allow the final coat to dry and fully harden for between one and two weeks.

TEST YOUR CHOSEN FINISH FIRST

Prepare offcuts of all of the woods used in the making of the guitar and bring them to the same level of polish as the woods on the main instrument. With any finish, it is advisable to try it out on these samples first to determine how successful it will be. Very oily woods such as rosewood and cocobolo can prevent an oil finish from drying properly and these tend to stay tacky. If this is the case, experiment with different oils, especially teak, as this can sometimes be more compatible with these woods.

TAKE CARE: IMPORTANT SAFETY NOTE

Cloths used for applying oil must be allowed to dry out laid flat. The oil in a scrunched up cloth can generate enough heat to self-combust. To be additionally safe, keep used cloths in an airtight container. If this sounds a bit far-fetched and you are wondering if I am pulling your leg, I can assure you I'm not. This has happened to someone I know, and his workshop was gutted and he lost everything!

Another phrase you may have heard with respect to finishing is 'fat over lean'. Essentially this means starting with thin light coats and perhaps progressing to slightly heavier subsequent layers once a good foundation has been established. In other words, don't hope that putting on a thick heavy layer initially will save time and result in less applications. The reverse is usually true and you may be left with an unsightly, gloopy mess that will require a lot of cutting back to rectify.

Polishing

To polish, the whole of the instrument's surface can be very lightly rubbed using 0000-grade wire wool. Alternatively, use the finest grades of Micro-Mesh abrasives, starting with 6000, then 8000 and finishing with 12000. Wipe over with a clean cloth between abrasive grades.

The whole surface can now be coated with lemon oil, which will help to prevent obvious fingerprints on the oiled surface. To finish, polish the instrument with a rough natural cloth such as hessian or burlap.

An offcut of
figured mahogany,
fully smoothed and
coated with Tru-Oil.

CHAPTER SEVEN

SETTING UP

Congratulations! You have now got to the stage where you can make your instrument speak. This can be a very exciting prospect, but as with all of the different steps your guitar has gone through so far, a bit of care and patience will be truly beneficial to the final result.

Make sure that the guitar is on a padded and secure surface to avoid any danger of it being scratched or knocked whilst carrying out the following operations.

Fitting The Hardware

The Machineheads

Check to see if any of the finish has built up in the machine-head roller holes. If so, carefully run the correct-sized drill bit down them to clean them out.

Mount the machineheads and check that they are square and in line with each other. Mark the screw holes with a sharp hard pencil, remove the heads and indent the centre of these marks with a bradawl. Choose a drill bit slightly smaller than the diameter of the screws and drill pilot holes, being careful to bore just deep enough for the screw lengths and no more. A piece of tape on the drill bit can act as a useful depth stop.

On slotted headstocks, be particularly careful that you do not drill right through the outer wall of the slot and also that the screws are short enough not to break through. If they are over-long, they will need to be ground down in length.

OPPOSITE PAGE:
Guitar #1: The slotted headstock complete with machineheads.

INSERTING SHORTENED SCREWS

If it becomes necessary to shorten the screws, they will end up with blunt ends. Drive an unmodified screw down each hole first to establish a thread, and then the shortened screws can be guided in more easily.

Remount the machineheads, then insert and drive home all screws using the correct screwdriver. Be aware that the wrong type can damage the screw heads and also there is a danger that a badly fitting driver could slip out and damage the guitar's finish.

A depth stop made with tape to avoid drilling machinehead screw holes too deeply.

Making the Nut and Saddle

The material that the nut and saddle are made of can make a big difference to the final sound of your guitar. Some cheaper mass-produced guitars come equipped with plastic moulded nuts that are often hollow and invariably changing them to a good quality, solid, hard material can improve the guitar's sound by quite a degree. The fit of the nut and saddle also affects the transfer of tone and vibration, so extra care should be taken to ensure that they are made to fit the slot provided precisely.

The material of choice for many makers is bone, which works well because of its inherent density and hardness. However, you may have a moral problem with using this due to its source, so there are several other alternatives. Luthier supply companies will sell you nut and saddle material such as Micarta®, Tusq®, Galalith® or Corian®. These are all synthetics that have been used with great success and will be superior to cheaper moulded plastic versions. You can also get nuts and saddles made of mother of pearl, or even brass. It is worth experimenting with different materials to find the one that suits your needs.

Making the Nut Blank

Cut a nut blank oversize and overlong. To flatten and smooth the rough-sawn faces of the blank use a flat file or, better still, sand it on a block of wood that has abrasive glued to it. (If the block has a coarse paper and a fine paper glued to either side, then the blank can be shaped on the rough side and smoothed on the fine.) Hold the sanding block steady by mounting it in a vice, so that you can concentrate on levelling the nut's surfaces.

Flatten one of the wider faces, which will be the side that sits against the end of the fingerboard. Next flatten the opposite face so that the nut blank can fit snugly between the fingerboard end and the back of the nut slot, which is formed by the angled edge of the headstock veneer. Be sure to keep the sides of the blank parallel and square.

Ensure that that is no glue squeeze-out in the bottom of the nut slot, and that it is clean, square and parallel.

Flatten the bottom edge of the nut blank, so that it sits perfectly onto the floor of the nut slot. You need to end up with a blank that sits securely in the slot and will not tip backwards and forwards.

The nut blank installed and a string slot level marked on with a half-pencil.

With the nut blank in its slot, run a half-pencil (cut in half longitudinally) across the first few frets and draw a line with it on the face of the nut blank. This will represent the height of the first fret and will be a guide as to where the slots should almost reach. Mark a further line 2mm (⁵⁄₆₄in) above this, following the curve of the fingerboard's camber, and cut off to this second line. Mark the exact width of the nut and trim down to size.

Making the Saddle Blank

Cut a saddle blank oversize and overlong. To flatten and smooth the rough-sawn faces of the blank use a flat file or, better still, sand it on a block of wood that has abrasive glued to it. Hold the sanding block steady by mounting it in a vice, so that you can concentrate on levelling the saddle's surfaces.

Flatten one of the wider faces, which will be the side that sits to the front of the saddle slot in the bridge. Flatten the opposite face so that the saddle blank can fit closely into the saddle slot. Be sure to keep the blank's sides parallel and square. Round off one end of the saddle blank to the same shape as the routed saddle slot end. Cut the blank slightly over length, and similarly round off the other end until the blank can be pushed into the slot.

Now flatten the bottom edge of the saddle blank, so that it sits perfectly onto the bottom of the saddle slot. You need to end up with a blank that sits securely in the slot and will not tip backwards and forwards.

THE IMPORTANCE OF A GOOD-FITTING SADDLE

A common problem with poor sound transference from the strings to the bridge and soundboard occurs due to poorly fitting saddles. Therefore, a flat-bottomed saddle slot and a similarly flat-bottomed saddle are essential for best results. The saddle should also be a push fit – not a hammer fit, but also not so loose that it can drop out if upturned.

Finally, mark where the saddle protrudes above the surface of the bridge, remove the saddle blank and draw a second line

The saddle blank being fitted.

approximately 3mm (⅛in) above the first. Cut off any excess above this second line.

Creating the Bridge Pin Holes

Drill out each of the bridge pin pilot holes with a 4mm (⁵⁄₃₂in) drill bit. Drill right through the soundboard and the bridge plate, but be careful not to force the drill through too quickly, as this will result in a frayed hole on the inside.

Depending on the bridge pins you intend to use, these holes need to be shaped with a reamer of the correct taper, either 3 or 5 degrees. This will allow the pins to locate and hold the string ends tightly.

Carefully twist the tapered reamer in each hole, taking off only very fine shavings and checking regularly with one of the bridge pins for a good fit. Most pins have a collar just below the domed head. Ream until the bridge pin collar just touches the surface of the bridge, and it is still a close fit.

Routing the Saddle Slot in Situ

Some makers prefer to rout the saddle slot once the bridge has been glued on to the soundboard. In this way, they can ensure that the saddle will be in the precise location for the best intonation. If this method is chosen, a way has to

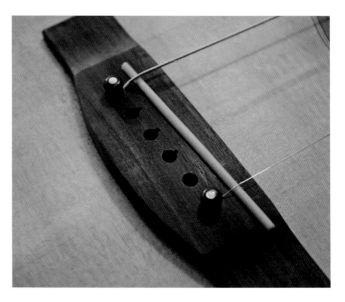

A temporary saddle with the top and bottom strings installed.

be devised to safely and accurately locate a router over the bridge, to enable it to fashion a consistent saddle slot. Jigs for this purpose can be bought, or a workshop-built one can be made (*see* photo opposite for one in action).

First, a temporary saddle has to be employed, for which a piece of hardwood or scrap saddle material can be used, cut to the correct thickness and height to replicate the final permanent saddle. Round the top to give the strings a positive contact point. You will also require an accurate electronic guitar tuner to ascertain good pitch.

Cut the nut slots as described later in this section and string up the guitar. Place the false saddle in approximately the right position and tune the top 'e' and bottom 'E' strings to pitch.

Play a harmonic on the top 'e' string and then fret it at the twelfth fret (consult the tuner to see if both notes correspond). If the fretted note is sharp, the string length needs to be increased, so push the temporary saddle back slightly towards the bridge pins (you may need to detune to achieve this). If it is reading flat, then the string length needs to be shortened, so push the saddle slightly forwards towards the neck and recheck. Repeat until the harmonic and the fretted note are identical. When they correspond, mark either side of that end of the saddle.

Replicate this with the bottom 'E' string, until the position of the end of the saddle is correct. Make sure that when moving this end it does not disturb the treble end of the saddle that you previously set up. When you are satisfied that

Reaming the holes to fit the bridge pins: note the use of tape as a marker.

A saddle slot being cut with a mini router on a purpose-built jig.

the bass end is correct, mark the position either side of the saddle.

If a continuous one-piece saddle is to be used, then this method is sufficient to place it accurately on the bridge.

Set up the jig so that the router will start the cut at one end of its slot in the place marked and end at the other mark. Rout a slot 4mm (⁵⁄₃₂in) deep, but cut in 1mm (³⁄₆₄in) increments.

Installing the Strings at the Bridge

The ball ends of the strings are required to sit securely up against the bridge plate under the bridge, held in place by the bridge pin shaft. Putting a slight kink in the string at the ball end will help it to be directed forward whilst the pin is inserted. Push the ball end down through the bridge hole, and hold the string securely in place while you insert the bridge pin. This will ensure that the pin does not drag the ball end further into the guitar, but directs it forward against the bridge plate.

Most bridge pins have a slot running up the side of the shaft, which allows clearance for the string. If not, it is possible

to cut a slot in the front of the tapered pin hole with a small file or small saw blade. You can also get sets of small round files that are designed for cleaning out the nozzles of welding torches and these work very well for this operation.

Sawing string slots in the bridge pin holes.

Cutting the Nut Slots

Each string slot should be the correct width for each string; wide enough for it to move through it without snagging whilst being tuned up, but not so wide that it moves excessively from side to side when plucked. Specialist nut files are available and are highly recommended for this operation. They can be expensive, but they will pay for themselves if they are also used for a few repair jobs.

The slots themselves should not run parallel to the top of the nut but slope down slightly towards the headstock angle. This will help to hold the string down in its slot and prevent excessive string bounce in the slot when it vibrates. The angle should be shallower than the headstock angle, so that as the string leaves the slot it is pulled down once again to its machinehead roller.

The string needs to be stopped exactly at the fingerboard side of the nut, so it is very important that each slot is flat along its length and not curved or bumpy. If the string only touches on the slot some way into the nut, this will throw out the intonation.

In a set of strings for a steel-string guitar the diameter of each string varies quite considerably, so if the nut slot centres were equi-spaced, the fatter-wound strings would be closer together than the plain thin strings. Therefore, the strings should be spaced evenly across the nut's width (that is, with equal space between the strings, not their centres). Specially designed string spacing rules are available, which

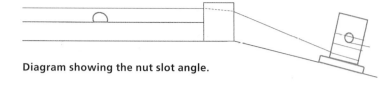

Diagram showing the nut slot angle.

have measurements that give you progressive slot spacing to compensate for the different string diameters from the treble to the bass. This obviously makes determining the spacing of the nut slots a lot easier, but if one is not available then it is possible to do it by eye.

Measure in from the treble end of the nut 3mm (⅛in) and mark this point as the centre of the top 'e' string slot. Similarly, mark in from the bass end of the nut 3mm (⅛in) and mark this point as the centre of the bottom 'E' string. Cut a shallow notch at these two points with the relevant nut file, of sufficient depth to allow the two outside strings to stay put when strung up.

String up the whole set: locate the two 'e' strings and space the remaining four strings evenly across the nut. When you are happy that the spacing looks right, pencil a line either side of the middle strings, detune and pull to one side. Cut shallow notches at these points with the relevant nut files, reposition the strings and tune up to pitch.

The nut slots now require cutting deeper until the strings are at the correct height for ease of playing, but not so low as to incur string buzz. This is often ascertained by measuring the distance between the bottom of each open/unfretted

Cutting the string slots in the nut.

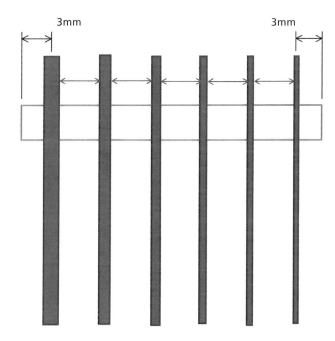

3mm   3mm

Diagram showing the nut string slot spacing.

until the correct height is achieved. This can be repeated for all strings.

ACHIEVING CORRECT NUT SLOT DEPTH

It is necessary to conduct this procedure of determining the correct string height, and therefore the necessary nut slot depth, with the strings at full concert pitch. If the strings were slack, they would not pull down into the slots sufficiently and you would get a false measurement.

When all the fret slots are at their correct depth, check the overall depth of the slots. Ideally the plain strings should sit flush with the top of the nut (so the depth of the slot is the same as the string's diameter) and the wound strings should sit halfway below the top of the nut (so the depth of the slot is half the string's diameter). If they exceed these dimensions,

string and the top of the first fret, but a common and reliable method is as follows. Press a string down at the third fret and observe the distance between the string and the top of the first fret. The string should just clear the first fret and not quite touch it. The nut slot for that string can then be lowered until this is achieved. Lift the string out of its slot, deepen the slot by a small amount, replace the string and recheck. Repeat

The nut string slots being initially filed.

The nut slots cut for the top and bottom strings.

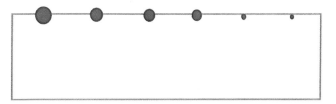

Diagram showing the string slot depths.

Lifting a string out of its slot with a specialist tool.

Thread the loose end of the string through the machine-head roller hole, but allow for a reasonable amount of slack by pulling up the middle of the string into an arch. Wind the string around the roller once *above* the free end in the hole, then start winding the machinehead, ensuring that the string then winds two or three times around, this time *under* the hole. This will direct the string downwards as it tunes to pitch. (*See* diagram showing the nut slot angle in the previous section.) Trim excess loose string to within 12.7mm (½in) of the roller.

WINDING STRINGS AROUND THE MACHINEHEAD ROLLERS

The thinner plain strings usually require three or four windings to stop them from slipping, while heavier wound strings only require two or three.

---

remove the nut and then grind the top surface of the nut until this is so.

Profile the back top edge of the nut into a curve (this reduces the friction on the string at the back of its slot) and polish out all scratches with fine abrasive. Spot a small amount of aliphatic glue on the fingerboard end, replace the nut and tune back up to pitch. This way the glue will hold the nut in place when future string changes are carried out, but the nut can still be removed by giving it a gentle tap with a hammer via a piece of wood.

Installing the Strings at the Machineheads

It is quite a surprise to discover how many people have very little idea of how the strings of a guitar should be installed into the machineheads. The most important aspect, as previously discussed, is that the string must leave the nut at an inclined angle to hold it down sufficiently in its slot to stop it bouncing.

Strings on a Solid Headstock

Ideally the string path should be a direct line from the back of the nut to the *bottom* of the machinehead roller. The easiest way to achieve this is as follows.

Strings on a Slotted Headstock

This has the advantage that the machinehead rollers are at the right level to pull the strings downwards. Thread the loose end of the string through the machinehead roller hole, but allow for a reasonable amount of slack by pulling up the middle of the string into an arch. Pull the loose end around the roller and thread it again through the hole. Hold the string under tension, and start winding the machinehead. For the outside strings, wind on the string such that the windings head towards the outside edge of the slot. For the middle four strings, send the windings towards the inside edge of the slot. Cut excess loose string to within 12.7mm (½in) of the roller.

Profiling the Saddle and Correcting the Intonation

The string must touch the top of the saddle at one point only. If the saddle top is flat then the string will not be defini-tively stopped and the intonation can be indeterminate. If the saddle top is curved then the string will have a far more positive contact point. The fret profiling file is very good for crowning the top of the saddle.

The top of the saddle should also follow the camber of the fingerboard. If, for instance, you have a 35.5cm (14in) radius

The saddle being carved for correct intonation.

on the fingerboard, then so should the saddle. If the saddle is too flat then the middle strings will end up too close to the fingerboard.

As previously discussed, the contact point can be adjusted over the thickness of the saddle. By filing from the back of the saddle, you can ramp the contact point to the front. By ramping from the front and the back, you can move the contact point to the centre of the saddle. Similarly, by filing from the front of the saddle, you can ramp the contact point to the back of the saddle.

The Saddle Height

Ideally, the string break angle from the saddle to the bridge pin should be the same as at the nut end, approximately 15 degrees. Therefore, it is important to achieve the correct height at which the saddle protrudes above the bridge. If too low (less than 2mm or ⁵⁄₆₄in) then the string break angle from the saddle to the bridge pins will be too shallow. This will have a detrimental effect on tone and volume, as the string will not be exerting enough downward pressure on the saddle/bridge to drive it efficiently. Conversely, if the saddle is too tall (more than 3mm) then the break angle starts to get too extreme. The saddle is then in danger of eventually

tipping forward and the strings are also putting excessive torque onto the bridge.

The bass strings generally require a little more clearance above the frets than the treble strings, so the saddle should be very slightly higher on the bass side than the treble. Measure the distance between the strings and the twelfth fret. A medium action reads at about 2.8mm (⁷⁄₆₄in) on the bass side and 2.0mm (⁵⁄₆₄in) on the treble.

Remember that the twelfth fret is at the halfway mark of the string length, so to lower the string height at this fret by 0.5mm you would have to lower the height of the saddle by 1.0mm.

Adjusting the Truss Rod

Sight along the neck from the nut end, or lay a straight edge along the frets to ascertain if the neck has pulled up into a significant up-bow with the strings at full tension. Normally there should be a small amount of curvature to the neck, known as relief, which will avoid string buzz if the action is on the low side. Hold down a string on the first fret, and also at the twelfth fret, to see if the string clears the sixth fret. There should be a very small gap between this fret and the bottom of the string. If it is excessive, then the truss rod needs adjusting to straighten the neck. If there is no gap at all, it may be that the truss rod needs adjusting the other way to release some tension to allow the strings to pull the neck up slightly.

For most truss rods, turning clockwise tightens the adjuster nut and this will straighten the neck. Conversely, turning anti-clockwise loosens the nut and will allow the neck to pull up into a curve. There is a common saying to remember this by: 'righty tighty, lefty loosy' (I'm sorry, but I did not make this up, so cannot be held responsible for it).

The Excitement of Those First Notes

Congratulations! You have before you an amazing creation, which will have invested in it hours of your time, dedication

Guitar #1: Left-handed with a slotted headstock, mahogany and ebony.

Guitar #2: Right-handed with a solid headstock, cherry and rosewood.

and sweat but hopefully not too many tears. You are now in possession of an instrument that you have nurtured, cajoled into being and possibly fought with for some time. I trust that it has not been an unhappy experience, but instead a period of great learning and a chance to gain an appreciation of the amount of work and thought that goes into guitar-making.

No matter how many guitars you make, there is nothing quite like that moment when you play those first notes and your new instrument talks to you. Despite meticulous attention to detail and the careful tuning of components, there is always that element of uncertainty and consequent anticipation and excitement about how it is going to perform. Remember that all of the components that go to make up a guitar have never before been asked to bear the particular stresses and strains that they now find themselves under. It all needs to settle, and it is not unusual to find yourself adjusting the truss rod, re-cutting the nut slots and so on to get the feel and the performance you require.

Because of this, don't expect everything to be at its optimum until a period of tweaking has passed. More than once I have found myself coming back to a new instrument the day after it has been completed and have been amazed at the improvement a few hours of settling in has achieved. It has been argued that the best guitars build up to their prime over time, opening up and finding their true voice. Give it time and enjoy playing your new creation, whilst planning what you are going to make next.

Maintenance and Repairs

Possibly without realising it, by learning the skills of guitar-making you have conjointly learnt many maintenance and repair techniques. Although these newfound skills may need further practise to perfect, the following common maintenance and repair jobs are now within your realm of expertise.

Customizing the Set-Up

In these days of the Internet, a lot of people buy instruments directly from the web. Unfortunately, as they are often bought unseen, they cannot be tried first. I regularly have guitarists bringing me new guitars that they are unhappy with because they are not set up to their requirements. Setting up a new guitar is normally a relatively simple task, which involves truss rod adjustment, string height adjustment (achieved by lowering the nut slots, altering the height of the saddle and so on) and correcting intonation problems.

Fret Dressing and Re-Frets

This may be necessary on new guitars where the fret installation has been less than perfect, or on older instruments that have frets that are pitted and worn due to playing wear.

Uneven frets gives rise to complaints from customers of string buzz.

When the frets are worn too far for a redress, possibly because the instrument has already had one or two before, or the frets are so badly worn that there is no hope of levelling them sufficiently whilst retaining adequate fret wire height, then a re-fret will be required. It is sometimes possible to do partial re-frets – it can sometimes be fairly obvious that some musicians only play down by the nut area and very seldom venture up to the 'dusty end'. It is not unusual to be presented with a guitar that has the first four or five frets completely worn out and the rest like new. In such cases replacing these first few frets, and then levelling and re-dressing them, is normally sufficient.

Nuts

Nuts can sometimes become over-worn or even broken and so require complete renewal. The slots could be badly cut so that the strings are not being stopped cleanly, which can create a buzz or sound a bit like a sitar, and this can often be rectified by simply re-cutting them. As has been discussed in Chapter 7, they could be of such an inferior material that replacing them can only enhance the guitar's sound.

Saddles

Saddles can also become over-worn or broken and so require complete renewal. They could be badly shaped, so that the strings are not being stopped cleanly, giving a buzz. Also, if they are not entirely flat along their bottom edges the fit will not be consistent on the bottom of the routed saddle slot. As with nuts, they could also be of such an inferior material that replacing them will enhance the guitar's sound.

Many guitar makers supplement their earnings by taking on repairs. It never ceases to amaze me how many guitarists there are out there, and they will always need work doing to their instruments, whether for a general set-up or a complete neck reset. Undertaking repairs will also justify and most probably pay for all of those specialist tools you have convinced yourself that you needed to make your first few guitars.

A NOTE FROM THE AUTHOR

Confession Time

I always encourage my students to detail in their written reports where things went wrong in their guitar-making, and what they did to rectify it. Well, in the pursuit of fairness, I had better do the same.

It may come as a surprise to some that even seasoned makers are only human! Real life can often intervene and things do not always go to plan. My hope is that by confessing to mistakes and explaining how they were resolved or 'covered up' you will feel better about mishaps that may have occurred during your making experience.

First, a Bit of Background

When I first agreed to write this book the plan was to make a guitar, and photograph and document the complete process. My main motivation for doing it was to allow me to get back into more making, as I spend most of my time these days teaching. I also decided that, as I invariably make guitars for others and have never had the luxury of making myself a steel-string guitar before, I would like to end up keeping the instrument for myself. This left the thorny issue of the guitar having to be left-handed – and wouldn't that be unfair on the right-handed readers of this tome?

Leaving aside the fact that us poor downtrodden south-paws have to convert everything we learn shown in the right-handed way, it was my dear wife who came to the rescue and suggested that I make two guitars, one left-handed and one right-handed. Brilliant! A great solution, albeit one that instantly doubled my workload. It did turn out to be an inspired idea, however, as it also gave me a perfect platform with which to demonstrate how the same basic model of guitar can look very distinctive by using different woods, headstock designs, cutaways and so on.

The workload issue was partly resolved by an inspired decision from me. One of my students was looking desperately for work experience and all of the usual avenues to work providers had gone strangely quiet. 'Come and work for me – I have a great project you could be involved in,' I suggested, and he foolishly agreed. Andrew made a lot of Guitar #2, but it was not without its problems.

What Went Wrong on the Guitars Detailed in This Book

I had found in my workshop a very nice pair of figured maple sides and a back that I'd had for many years and suggested that Guitar #2 should be made with these. The back was dutifully joined and prepared, and came out well. Unfortunately, the sides were a nightmare to bend; they cracked in so many places that in the end we decided to abandon them. I instead sourced a good but plain back and sides of cherry, which worked and bent very well, and ended up looking good.

A back and sides of figured mahogany that again I had stashed away in my workshop I decided were destined for Guitar #1. They were very attractive, with fiddle-back type figuring, and I reasoned that they would make a stunning-looking instrument. Unfortunately, by the time I got to prepare them and bend the sides, I realized that it was going to be quite a fight. The distinct figuring meant that the only way I could smooth them was by using a very sharp scraper plane, and only then at exactly the right angle to the figure. The sides when bent went every-which-way, most likely due to the way they had been cut from the log. This can be the downside of highly figured timbers – they look good but they can be very unstable. Although I eventually beat them into submission, in the end the sides are not exactly flat across their width, even with rib supports on the inside. The fact that this is going to be my guitar resolves this problem somewhat, but I would not have been happy if this was a guitar I was making for someone else.

The back for Guitar #1 was braced during a period of cold, damp weather and unfortunately had to be left for a couple of weeks before fitting to the ribs. Although it was secured in the go-bar deck under pressure, the day assigned for fitting turned out to be an unseasonably hot April day, and when released from the deck the braces very quickly reverted from what was a nice convex arch to a concave one.

A cure for this is sometimes possible, by placing the back in a sealed plastic bag that contains a small bowl of water.

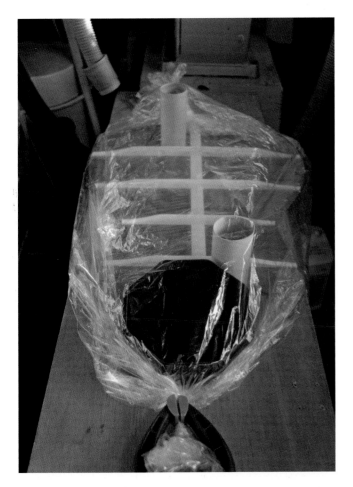

An attempt to correct an arch in the back after an unseasonably hot period.

The principle is that eventually the braces will absorb enough moisture to transform back to their original profile.

On this occasion this did not work, however, and it was necessary to chisel off the original braces. If you do this, be very careful not to damage the back's surface. Clean up any old glue with a sharp scraper and replace the warped braces with new ones that have been contoured and glued on in the changed atmospheric conditions.

When it came to routing the back binding channel for both guitars, I was modifying the router base to allow it to run off the rib sides but only touch a small point on the back to compensate for the arched plate. It worked very well on the whole, apart from on Guitar #2 where it slipped near the tail and created a bit of a divot in the rib. To overcome this, I inlaid an extra piece of binding either side of the tail graft. I also managed to rout a bit too deep for the bindings that I had. This was rectified by gluing on two lines of purfling before the binding went on.

The moral of these stories is, if you are going to experiment and modify, be careful about doing it on a customer's instrument. Also, if you are going to make a mistake, make it look as if it was intentional.

Each instrument will be different and will throw up its own challenges that have to be overcome, sometimes with ingenious solutions. One of the curses of being a maker is that sometimes when looking over a guitar you have just made you can only see the things that did not go to plan. However, I can assure you that this will pass – unless you are an out-and-out perfectionist, in which case you will probably never be entirely satisfied with what you have achieved. Despite any trials and tribulations, I sincerely hope that this book has inspired you to make more guitars.

The braces removed and all traces scraped clean.

GLOSSARY

000-style A body size designation introduced by Martin.

back The rear plate that is braced into a gentle dome to give the body structural integrity and also to radiate the guitar's vibrations out through the soundhole.

back graft The light but strong strip that strengthens the back's centre join.

binding The edging of hardwood that protects the vulnerable edges of the soundboard and back.

brace A light but strong piece of quarter-sawn timber that gives either the soundboard or the back structural integrity.

bridge A shaped block of hardwood that houses the saddle and also anchors one end of all of the strings. It serves to radiate the strings' vibrations to the soundboard. It should also be considered to be a further soundboard brace, so the bigger its footprint and bulk the more it will restrict the soundboard's vibrations.

bridge pin The tapered peg that holds the string end, which is anchored to the bridge.

bridge plate A plate of hardwood that is glued directly under the bridge on the reverse side of the soundboard. It serves to protect the soft wood of the soundboard from being damaged by the string ball ends. It also gives the bridge some extra strength to resist the considerable tension from the strings.

caul A wooden block that is inserted between a clamp and the component being glued, to prevent damage and to spread the clamping pressure.

cleats Small thin squares of quarter-sawn spruce that are glued across the soundboard join as insurance against it opening up due to extremes of humidity.

datum face A surface from which all further measurements are taken.

dished workboard A wooden disc that has a shallow hollowed top surface that conforms to the same radius as the soundboard or back.

Dremel A make of mini power tool, used for routing and shaping.

end graft A piece of decorative inlay inset at the tail end of the body where the ribs join.

fan brace A system of braces commonly used on 'classical' nylon-strung guitars, where five to seven thin low-profile braces radiate or fan back from the bridge position.

finger braces Small low-profile braces that radiate up and towards the waist from the lower X-brace arms.

fingerboard A hardwood topping to the neck that carries the frets, commonly stretching from the nut to the soundhole.

fingerboard patch A low-profile patch of wood that is glued across the fingerboard extension area under the soundboard.

fret A domed metal wire onto which the strings are pressed down when a note requires raising or lowering in pitch.

fret tang The part of the fret that is inlaid into the fingerboard.

go-bar deck A strong framework that has a dished workboard at the base on which a soundboard or back can have its braces glued by means of sticks that are bent between the brace and the roof of the deck.

headstock A section at the top of the neck that contains the machineheads, which tune the strings to pitch.

headstock veneer A decorative thin wood facing to the headstock.

heel cap A decorative cap of thin wood on the bottom of the neck heel.

intonation The capability of playing a note in tune.

lining A wooden strip affixed to the top and bottom edges of the ribs to allow a greater gluing surface for the soundboard and back.

lower bout The area of the lower part of the guitar that encompasses the bridge.

luthier Originally a term used to describe a maker of lutes, but more widely used these days for stringed instrument makers.

machinehead A mechanical tuner with a roller onto which the string ends are wound.

neck block A substantial block of wood mounted at the top end of the guitar to which the neck is affixed.

nut A string spacer and string stop at the top of the neck at the end of the fingerboard.

position markers A dot or block marker inlayed into the surface of the fingerboard to denote certain fret positions.

purfling Decorative veneer lines inlaid commonly between the soundboard and its binding.

radius (of the fingerboard) The curvature of the surface of the fingerboard.

re-fret The replacement of some or all of the frets due to wear or for substitution by frets of an alternative size.

ribs The bent rims to which the soundboard and the back are fixed that form the sides of the soundbox.

rub joint A form of joint where one half of the joint has glue applied and then the other half is rubbed back and forth on it until the glue begins to grab. It is then left to set when precisely in position.

quarter sawn Wood cut from a log that has its end grain running at right angles to its surface.

saddle An insert into the bridge that raises the strings to a correct playing height and a string length stop.

shooting (edges) The process of running a plane along the long thin edges of soundboards and backs prior to joining their halves together.

side dots A dot or marker inlaid into the edge of the fingerboard to denote certain fret positions.

soundboard The guitar's top plate.

soundbox The complete instrument body made up from the ribs, back and soundboard.

soundhole The hole in the soundboard from which the sound emanates.

soundhole inlay Inlaid lines and decoration around the soundhole's circumference.

tack cloth A cloth impregnated with linseed oil that is used to wipe a surface to remove all traces of dust.

tail block A wooden block at the lower end of the guitar's body where the two ribs join.

tear-out Where the grain of the wood rises to the surface at a contrary angle to the direction of cut from a plane, resulting in wood shards tearing out of the surface.

thicknesser A machine or jig that reduces a piece of timber to a consistent thickness when it is passed through it.

tone bars These are like braces but their main purpose is to influence the soundboard's tone and they are often placed to balance the response of the soundboard.

tonewoods Woods commonly selected for instrument-making because of their superior acoustic properties.

transverse brace This brace defines a border between the mostly resonant lower half of the soundboard and the largely non-resonant top section where the fingerboard extension and neck join reside.

truss rod Metal threaded rod(s) embedded in the neck that is designed to adjust the flatness of the neck.

twelve-fret The point at which the neck joins the body on this type of instrument.

upper bout The area of the upper part of the guitar.

waist The area of the middle part of the guitar where the ribs curve inwards.

X-brace The main supporting brace for the soundboard consisting of two arms that intersect, forming an X.

SUGGESTED FURTHER READING

There is an enormous amount of information related to musical instrument making on the internet. There are also many books and DVDs available about the subject, a small selection of which are detailed below.

Books

Benedetto, Robert, *Making an Archtop Guitar* (E. Stroudsburg, Pa: Limelite Press, 1994).

Courtnall, Roy, *Making Master Guitars* (London: Hale, 1993).

Cumpiano, William R. and Natelson, Jonathan D., *Guitar Making: Tradition and Technology* (San Francisco: Chronicle Books, 1994).

Erlewine, Dan, *Guitar Player Repair Guide* (Stewart MacDonald, 2007).

Erlewine, Dan and MacRostie, Don, *Guitar Finishing: Step by Step* (Stewart MacDonald, 1998).

Erlewine, Dan, *Fret Work: Step by Step* (Stewart MacDonald, 1993).

Evans, Tom and Evans, Mary, *Guitars: Music, History, Construction and Players from the Renaissance to Rock* (New York: Paddington Press, 1977).

Flexner, Bob, *Flexner on Finishing* (Ohio: Popular Woodworking Books, 2010).

Hiscock, Melvyn, *Make Your Own Acoustic Guitar* (Dunsford, Surrey: NBS Publications, 2010).

Hurd, David, *Left-Brain Lutherie* (Bold Strummer Ltd, 2004).

Johnston, R. and Boak, D., *Martin Guitars: A Technical Reference* (New York: Hal Leonard Books, 2009).

Johnston, R. and Boak, D., *Martin Guitars: A History* (New York: Hal Leonard Books, 2008).

Kinkead, Jonathan, *Build Your Own Acoustic Guitar* (London: Batsford, 2004).

Manson, Andy, *Talking Wood: A Guitar Maker's Diary* (Tiverton: R&D Associates, 1998).

Middleton, Rik, *The Guitar Maker's Workshop* (Marlborough: Crowood, 1997).

Noonan, Jeffrey J., *The Guitar in America: Victorian Era to Jazz Age* (University Press of Mississippi, 2008).

Ramirez III, José, *Things About the Guitar*, (Madrid: Soneto, 1993).

Robinson, Larry, *The Art of Inlay* (Backbeat Books, 2005).

Romanillos, José, *Antonio de Torres: Guitar Maker – His Life and Work* (Shaftesbury: Element Books, 1987).

Siminoff, Roger, *Luthier's Handbook* (Hal Leonard Corporation, 2007).

Siminoff, Roger, *Tap Tuning* (Hal Leonard Corporation, 2007).

Sloane, Irving, *Steel String Construction* (Westport, CT: Bold Strummer, 1990).

Sloane, Irving, *Classic Guitar Construction* (Westport, CT: Bold Strummer, 1989).

Somogyi, Ervin, *The Responsive Guitar* (Luthiers Press, 2010).

Teagle, John, *Washburn: Over One Hundred Years of Fine Stringed Instruments* (New York: Music Sales Corporation, 1996).

Turnball, Harvey, *The Guitar from the Renaissance to the Present Day* (Westport, CT: Bold Strummer, 1991).

Tyler, James, *The Early Guitar: A History and Handbook* (London: Oxford University Press, 1980).

Tyler, James and Sparks, Paul, *The Guitar and its Music: From the Renaissance to the Classical Era* (New York: Oxford University Press, 2002).

Willis, Alex, *Step-by-Step Guitar Making* (Guild of Master Craftsman Publications, 2010).

DVDs

Erlewine, Dan, *Fret Basics* (Stewart MacDonald).

Everett, Kent, *Adjusting a Steel String Guitar* (Apprentice Publishing).

Everett, Kent, *Voicing a Steel String Guitar* (Apprentice Publishing).

Fernandez, Ronald, *French Polishing for Guitarmakers* (Fernandez Music).

MacRostie, Don, *Sunburst Finishing* (Stewart MacDonald).

MacRostie, Don and Erlewine, Dan, *Spray Finishing Basics* (Stewart MacDonald).

Somogyi, Ervin, *Voicing the Guitar* (Luthiers Press).

SUPPLIERS

Luthier Suppliers

Touchstone Tonewoods
44 Albert Road North, Reigate, Surrey, RH2 9EZ
Tel: 01737 221064
Web: www.touchstonetonewoods.co.uk
Wood. tools, hardware, strings and so on.

David Dyke Luthiers Supplies
The Hall, Horebeech Lane, Horam, Heathfield, East Sussex,
TN21 0HR
Tel: 01435 812315
Web: www.luthierssupplies.co.uk
Wood, tools, hardware, strings and so on.

Tonetech Luthier Supplies
Unit 4/6A Meadow Mill, Water Street, Stockport, SK1 2BU
Tel: 0161 429 6955
Web: www.tonetechluthiersupplies.co.uk

Timberline
Units 7 and 11A, Munday Works, 58–66 Morley Road,
Tonbridge, Kent, TN9 1RP
Tel: 01732 355626
Web: www.exotichardwoods.co.uk
*All types of timber, also specialist musical instrument timber,
inlays and veneers, tools.*

Stewart Macdonalds Guitar Shop Supply
Box 900, Athens, Ohio 45701, USA
Web: www.stewmac.com
Email: intl@stewmac.com
*A vast range of specialist guitar-making tools, timber and
supplies.*

Allied Lutherie
P.O. Box 217, 498A Moore Lane, Healdsberg, CA, 95448, USA
Web: www.alliedlutherie.com
Email: sales@alliedlutherie.com

Luthiers Mercantile International
P.O. Box 774/412 Moore Lane, Healdsburg, CA 95448, USA
Web: www.lmii.com
Email: lmi@lmii.com
Specialist guitar-making timbers, tools and supplies.

Dick GmbH
Donaustr.51. 94526 Metten, Germany.
Web: www.dick-gmbh.de
Email: info@dick-gmbh.de
Luthiers' supplies, tools and so on.

Inlays and Veneers

Philip A. Cheshire Ltd
Inlay Works, Vale Road, London, N4 1TS
Tel: 020 8 809 4484
Web: www.philipacheshire.co.uk
Inlays.

J. Crispin & Sons Ltd
12 & 13 Gemini Business Park, Hornet Way, Beckton,
London, E6 7FF
Tel: 020 7 474 3680
Email: info@capitalcrispin.co
Web: www.capitalcrispin.com
Veneers, inlays.

Abbey Marquetry
Tasma Products, Unit 1, College Farm, Meldreth, Royston,
Herts. SG8 6NT
Tel: 01763 260716
Veneers, inlays.

Art Veneers
Industrial Estate, Mildenhall, Suffolk, IP28 7AY
Tel: 01638 712330
Web: www.artveneers.co.uk
Veneers, inlays.

Finishing Supplies

A.P.Fitzpatrick
142 Cambridge Heath Road, Bethnal Green, London E1 5QJ
Tel: 020 7 790 0884
Web: www.apfitzpatrick.co.uk
Art materials, animal glue, varnish, finishing supplies.

Foxell and James
57 Farringdon Road, London, EC1M 3JB
Tel: 020 7 405 0152
Art materials, varnish, finishing supplies.

Tools and Machinery

Axminster Power Tool Centre Ltd
Unit 10 Weycroft Avenue, Axminster, Devon, EX13 5PH
Tel: 0800 371822
Web: www.axminster.co.uk
*An extremely comprehensive range of general hand tools,
machinery, some inlays and veneers and so on.*

Tilgear
Langley House, Station Road, Standon, Herts SG11 1QN
Tel: 0845 0990220
Web: www.tilgear.info
*A comprehensive range of general hand tools, machinery and
so on.*

Classic Hand Tools
Unit 8, Hill Farm Business Park, Witnesham, Suffolk, IP6 9EW
Web: www.classichandtools.com
Email: sales@classichandtools.co.uk
*A comprehensive range of tools, including Dictum tools, Pfeil
carving tools, Vallorbe musical instrument-making tools, Veritas
and Lie-Nielsen tools.*

Buck and Ryan
Shop 4, Victoria House, Southampton Row, London, WC1
4DA
Web: www.buckandryan.co.uk
Tel: 020 7 430 9898
A comprehensive range of hand tools and machinery.

INDEX

000 style 12, 36

A
abrasive paper 13

B
back /2–76, 87–91
back braces 75, 87–88
bending iron 76
binding 99–111
bridge 137–145
bridge pins 158–159
bridge plate 95–96

C
cauls 20
chisels 15–18
clamping technique 20
Cutaway Florentine 79
Cutaway Venetian 78

D
diamond stone 16
dished workboard 72, 87
Dremel 102, 137

E
end graft 83
end grain 20
Engelmann spruce 12

F
fan brace 35
filler 148
finger brace 36–37, 92, 97
fingerboard 118–127

fingerboard extension wedge 123–125
fingerboard patch 36–37, 92, 97
fingerboard radius 126
finishing 147–153
flatness 19
French polishing 147
fret barber 131–132
fret bender 128–129
fret position markers 122–123
fret position side dots 122–123
frets 117–119, 127–137

G
glue 20, 27–30
gluing technique 13, 20, 29
go-bar deck 72, 87
grain runout 20

H
hand tools 15, 21, 22–25
hardwoods 12
headstock 45, 49–55
Health and safety 22
heel 48, 60
heel cap 117
history 35
honing guide 16
humidity 30–31

I
intonation 140–144
inventive 13

J
jigs 32

L

lighting 13, 32
linings 81
luthier 10

M

machineheads 45, 155
machinery 21, 25–26
maintenance and repair 165
maker's label 91
materials 27–30
model type 11
moulds 32, 41–43

N

neck 45–61
neck angle 113–115
neck block 79, 84–85
neck joint mortice 84, 113–116
nut 45, 156–157, 160–162

O

oil finish 148, 151–153

P

patience 12
perfection 13
physical attributes 11
planes 15–17, 19–20
planing problems 20
planing technique 19–20
planning 12
plans 12
preparation 148
preparing a timber blank 21
purfling 99–111
purfling marker 100, 102

Q

quarter-sawn 30

R

reinforcement cleats 97–98
rib strengthening strips 82
ribs 76–79, 81
router 48, 100

S

saddle 156–159, 163
scrapers 13, 18–19
setting up 155–164
sharpening 15–17
sharpness 12,
sitka spruce 12
soundboard 36, 61–72, 92–99
soundboard braces 72, 92–97
soundboard thickness 71–72
soundhole brace 36–37, 92
soundhole inlay 65–71
spool clamps 89–90
squareness 19
storage 31
straight edge 16
strings 159–163

T

tail block 80, 85
tearout 20
templates 32, 39–41, 43–44
tone bar 36–37, 92, 97
tonewoods 11
transverse brace 36–37, 92, 97
truss rod 48, 116–117, 163–164
twelve fret guitar 12

V

varnish 147, 151

W

water stone 16
wood storage 30
woods 11–12, 27, 30, 32–33, 44–45
working conditions 30–32
workspace 22

X

X-brace 35, 36, 92–94

OTHER CRAFT TECHNIQUE BOOKS FROM CROWOOD

Abbott, Kathy *Bookbinding*

Adcock, Sandra *Commercial Floristry – designs and techniques*

Brooks, Nick *Mouldmaking and Casting*

Brooks, Nick *Advanced Mouldmaking and Casting*

Burke, Ed *Glass Blowing*

Daniels, Chris *The Craft of Stonemasonry*

Ellen, Alison *Hand Knitting*

Ellen, Alison *Knitting – colour, structure and design*

Fish, June *Designing and Printing Textiles*

Goodwin, Elaine M. *The Human Form in Mosaic*

Grenier, Fleur *Pewter – designs and techniques*

Hunter, Andrea *Creating Felt Pictures*

Parkinson, Peter *The Artist Blacksmith*

Perkins, Tom *The Art of Letter Carving in Stone*

Richards, Ann *Weaving Textiles That Shape Themselves*

Seymour, Martin *Clinker Boat Building*

Smith, Alan *Etching*

Taylor, Chris *Leatherwork – a practical guide*

Thaddeus, Martin, and Thaddeus, Ed *Welding*

Tregidgo, Jan *Torchon Lacemaking – a step-by-step guide*

Waller, Jane *Knitting Fashions of the 1940s*

Watkins-Baker Helga *Kiln Forming Glass*

Werge-Hartley, Jeanne *Enamelling on Precious Metals*